IMAGES
of America

THE JEWISH COMMUNITY
of WASHINGTON, D.C.

Cantor William and Mrs. Jenny Tash had this picture taken on their wedding day in 1911. They were very giving people, and in order to make ends meet, the family took in boarders for a nominal charge and some of their children sold newspapers. (Courtesy of the Jewish Historical Society of Greater Washington.)

IMAGES
of America

THE JEWISH COMMUNITY
of WASHINGTON, D.C.

Dr. Martin Garfinkle
Introduction by Dr. Adam Garfinkle
Foreword by the Jewish Historical Society of
Greater Washington

ARCADIA
PUBLISHING

Published by Arcadia Publishing
Charleston, South Carolina

Library of Congress Catalog Card Number: 2005930279

For all general information contact Arcadia Publishing at:
Telephone 843-853-2070
Fax 843-853-0044
E-mail sales@arcadiapublishing.com
For customer service and orders:
Toll-Free 1-888-313-2665

Visit us on the Internet at www.arcadiapublishing.com

This book is dedicated to the memory of my great-grandfather and great-grandmother Morris and Annie Garfinkle of Blessed Memory; to Morris and Annie's great-great-grandsons Steven and Eric; to my daughter-in-law, Limor; and to my wife, Caryn.

The front cover of this book is a picture of the ceremony for laying the cornerstone of the Jewish Community Center of Washington, D.C., on May 3, 1925. Calvin Coolidge spoke prior to the cornerstone being put in place. This is a picture of the same cornerstone taken on May 7, 2005, 80 years later. (Photograph by Limor Garfinkle.)

CONTENTS

Morris and Annie Garfinkle *c.* 1943 recite the Kiddush at their home at 1424 Crittenden Street NW in Washington, D.C.

FOREWORD

The story line of Washington's Jewish community is often told rather one-dimensionally. Jews came late to the city, followed the usual patterns of immigration, opened small shops that grew into large stores, organized synagogues and Jewish communal organizations, and eventually spread to the suburbs.

Dr. Martin Garfinkle has added dimension to the story with this book. Drawing on a rich family archive of photographs, on the following pages, Dr. Garfinkle shows many images that have never been seen beyond his family circle. These photographs, with those from other libraries and archives including more than 30 from our own archive of the Jewish community at the Jewish Historical Society of Greater Washington, tell a story of the rich and textured life of the Garfinkle family and the Jewish community in which they lived, worked, and worshipped.

Garfinkle's personal story belies the fact that not all of Washington's Jews are transient as is often believed. Garfinkle is a fourth-generation Washingtonian, though he now lives in New York. His great-grandfather Morris Garfinkle arrived in D.C. by 1900, established a successful shoe business, and was involved in myriad local and national Jewish organizations.

On these pages, you will see the Washington that is hometown and nation's capital to the sixth-largest Jewish community in the United States. Incorporated in 1800, Washington had its first Jews begin arriving in earnest in the 1840s. Unlike New York, Boston, Philadelphia, and Charleston's Colonial Jewish communities, Washington, D.C., was cornfields and Indian hunting lands at the time these other cities were being developed. A creation of Congress, the community was late only because there was no town or city in which to settle.

Unlike other cities, Washington's first immigrants were from Central Europe. Eastern European Jews followed, and reversing the usual migration pattern, Sephardic Jews arrived in the 1920s. While many started in business with small shops—groceries, furniture stores, tailors, jewelers—the presence of the federal government had a profound effect. Their clientele included presidents, Supreme Court justices, and congressmen. The few who served in the federal government for the century preceding the New Deal gave way to a wave of young intellectuals who arrived to serve a burgeoning federal government in the 1930s and 1940s.

Continued growth and prosperity in the post–World War II era and into the modern era have created a community that spans three jurisdictions—D.C. and the Maryland and Northern Virginia suburbs—and includes more than 250,000 members.

The Jewish Historical Society of Great Washington is the nation's central archives for the special community. Our collections are open to researchers by appointment. Our programs and exhibits recount this unique history—at once local and national.

—Laura Cohen Apelbaum
Executive Director
Jewish Historical Society of Greater Washington
Lillian and Albert Small Jewish Museum
www.jhsgw.org

ACKNOWLEDGMENTS

I was looking to purchase a book on the Jewish community of Washington, D.C., having lived there for the first 20 years of my life. To my chagrin, nothing recent had been written except for David Altshuler's book, *The Jews of Washington, D.C.: A Communal History Anthology*, published in 1985, which was a wonderful reference tool for me. Rabbi Stanley Rabinowitz's book, *The Assembly: A Century In the Life of the Adas Israel Hebrew Congregation of Washington, D.C.*, published in 1993, was an excellent history book on Adas Israel Congregation. However, I did not find any publication that contained both a visual and written narrative on the Jewish founders of today's growing Jewish community. Since none existed, I had to write it.

My initial mentor who encouraged me to write this book was Jenny Tango, an Arcadia author who showed me the way to make this project come true. Others who supported me were my cousin, Adam Garfinkle, and Laura Cohen Apelbaum and Wendy Turman of the Jewish Historical Society of Greater Washington, who provided research assistance as well as many of the archival photographs seen throughout this book. My cousin Phyllis Lincoln sent me pictures from my great-uncle Ralph Garfinkle's archives. My editor, Kathryn Korfonta, was there for me whenever questions or problems arose. Both Sidney Berger and Erwin Garfinkle provided pictures and a wealth of personal knowledge and recollections on the Washington, D.C., Jewish community. And finally, my daughter-in-law, Limor Garfinkle, spent many hours taking photographs that can be seen throughout this book and provided technical assistance throughout the project.

My secondary team gave hours of their time helping in the research for this book. Without them, the task would have been too difficult to accomplish: Rabbi Shmuel Herzfeld, who opened the doors to Ohev Shalom Congregation; Rabbi Joel Tessler, who opened the doors to Beth Shalom Congregation; Celia Marszal, who did an extraordinary job in her research efforts; Ronald Schlesinger, for opening the doors of Adas Israel and who spent a Sunday with us doing a photo shoot; Rabbi Barry Freundel and congregants, who opened the doors to Kesher Israel Congregation; Mr. and Mrs. Leonard Goodman, who gave us two Sunday mornings so that we could access and do research in the Ohev Shalom archives; Mrs. Toby Berman from Beth Shalom Congregation, who gave us access to their archives; Jennifer King and her staff at the George Washington University Library Archives Division; the library staff at the Washington Hebrew Congregation; Cathy Allen at the Aeronautics Museum in College Park, Maryland; and Bill Burdick from the National Baseball Hall of Fame Library, Cooperstown, New York.

Thank you to my cheering team, without whose encouragement this book would not have been the joy that it was: Dr. Russ Hotzler, president of New York City College of Technology; Provost Bonne August; Deans Steven Soifer, Sonja Jackson, and Victor Ayala; Prof. Julia Jordan, who can light up a smile with her words "that's wonderful Marty"; Prof. Steven Panford for his encouragement and research efforts; and my brother Ronald Garfinkle for his contributions.

Finally thanks to my children who endured hours of discussion on this book, and last but not least, to my wife, Caryn, who is my number one supporter.

INTRODUCTION

The history of the Jewish people is an improbable one. No other people has survived the loss of its ancestral land, political sovereignty, and spoken language for nearly two millennia and then managed to reconstitute all three. In the course of this improbable history, Jews have wandered and lived throughout the world, and even today they dwell in many dozens of countries as distinct self-identified Jewish communities despite the establishment of the modern State of Israel. We do not know what the future will bring, but it would not be too much to claim that Jews have created the most successful transterritorial civilization in history. It is nothing short of a cumulative miracle.

It is therefore no surprise that Jews should be found in and around Washington, D.C., which the journalist Wade Hampton McCree once described as the only city in the world where sound travels faster than light. After all, one miracle deserves another.

Jews have been able to live, and often to live well, in so many different environments on account of three precious assets that defy physical rootedness: faith, family, and facility in professional and commercial life. Our faith has given us purpose and hope. Our families have given us support and consolation. Our facilities have given us sustenance and flexibility. And all three are illustrated by the history of the Jews of Greater Washington.

The community began small, as small as possible in fact, with the arrival of one Isaac Polock to Washington in 1795. Isaac arrived from Savannah with real estate speculation on his mind. We are not sure how well he did with property, but rumor has it that before long he was selling cigars to Aaron Burr and cleaning up at local whist tables.

In any event, the Jewish community of Washington, D.C., remained small for many decades, reaching a population of only 200 at the time of the Civil War. Most of Washington's Jewish community at that time had come up from farther south, from Savannah, New Orleans, and even Richmond, where German Jews who had left Europe with and after the Revolutions of 1848 had settled in substantial numbers. Among the community were a few Sephardic families, like the Cardoso family, some tracing their origins back to the first Jewish community in the New World at Pernambuco.

By 1880, just before the promulgation of the notorious May Laws in the Czarist Empire, the city's Jewish population had grown considerably, to about 1,500, the majority still of German-Jewish origin. But just 10 years later, the population had more than doubled, to about 3,500. Most of the new souls were Yiddish-speaking Jews coming from the troubled domains of the Russian Empire. Among these were Morris Garfinkle and Adam Luber, my paternal and maternal grandfathers, respectively.

Morris Garfinkle and his wife to be, Annie Minsky, had lived in New York City before coming to Washington. Adam Luber had come with his wife, Jenny, from the old country directly to Cedar Rapids, Iowa. For another clutch of unknown reasons, the Lubers soon headed off to Atlanta, Georgia, where their first child died of fever and no permission could be gotten to bury the body. They came to Washington soon thereafter.

These little anecdotes are useful for pointing out that every Jew in Washington came from somewhere else, because Washington had no port of entry for large ships from abroad. Jews were drawn to Washington by their already established family, by hope of new opportunities, by curiosity, or by as little as a wispy morning dream.

Characteristic of Jewish communities everywhere, the Jews of Washington lived near each other and, in their different origins, suspected and occasionally detested each other. Many of the earlier-settled German Jews were Reform Jews, but most of the newer arrivals remained Orthodox. They established synagogues; Al Jolson grew up in one of them. They established the ways and means for kosher slaughtering and baking. They established free-loan societies and other community organizations, including Zionist organizations. When the time came after December 1941, they with other Washington Jews joined the army, the navy, and the Marine Corps.

The more affluent Sephardic and German families, fluent English speakers by the mid-1880s, are said to have looked down at first upon their somewhat more exotically dressed and less wealthy East European brothers. Most of the newcomers went into various wholesale and retail trades along Seventh Street NW and environs. Morris Garfinkle founded a shoe-finding wholesale business near Seventh and I Streets, selling parts of shoes to those craftsmen who did repair work across the city. Adam Luber had a grocery store not far away that, as most did before Prohibition, also sold alcoholic beverages. (Just after the end of Prohibition in 1933, Adam Luber and a partner founded what came to be the largest liquor store in town, Central Liquor.)

In time, the community, in its diverse origins, found common bearings, but as the community expanded, it also lost some of its original tight-knitted sensibility. And expand it did, along with the city as a whole. Washington grew especially rapidly during and just after World War II. By 1951, the year that I was born, the Jewish population of Washington had mushroomed to more than 45,000. Newcomers now far out-numbered the original turn-of-the-century community and its blood descendants, and they spread hither and yon, out Sixteenth Street and Georgia Avenue and even into the Virginia suburbs. And so the Hebrew Home for the Aged, originally on Spring Road, moved to Rockville. So B'nai Israel, once on Sixteenth Street, did the same. So Posin's grocery and Hofberg's restaurant came, and so eventually they went.

And so it has continued. The community today reaches just around 200,000 souls and still expands outward into exurbia. So for all anyone knows, it will continue to do so all the way to Pikesville, Manassas, Harper's Ferry, and beyond.

I am a native, and though I was exiled to Philadelphia for three decades, I am now back. My parents were both born here before the great World War II influx. All four of my Yiddish-speaking grandparents lived here before the great hinge of the 19th century swung shut. I myself saw Camilo Pascual throw those great sweeping fall-off-the-table curve balls at Griffith Stadium, and I am so much still a Washington Senators fanatic that I make a kind of *yarhzeit* call nearest every December 10 to Walter Johnson's grave in Rockville Cemetery. I don't actually say *Kaddish* for him; but yes I admit it, I do think about it.

So if you are a native Jew from Washington, and especially if your family goes back as far in this place as mine does, you will be transported by the photographs and depictions my cousin Martin has labored to bring together in this fine book. You will treasure it because it will blend with your memories, with your life. You will show it to your children and grandchildren, if not today, then one day, and you will hope they feel as you feel when they see these images. Perhaps they will.

—Adam Garfinkle
June 1, 2005

Abraham Lincoln befriended two Washington Jews, Simon Wolf and Adolphus Solomons. Simon Wolf pleaded to Lincoln to save the life of a young deserter who left his regiment to visit his sick mother. During the Civil War, deserters were summarily tried by a military court and, if found guilty, were executed before a firing squad. Wolf successfully pleaded for the soldier's life, and a reluctant Lincoln stayed the execution; the boy was returned to his regiment. The "deserter" fought gallantly for his country and died in 1864 in the Battle of Cold Harbor. Lincoln also befriended Adolphus Solomons and the two became great friends. Solomons, in a book that he published about his life, claimed that he took the last photograph of Lincoln while alive, on April 9, 1865. The Washington Hebrew Congregation had the honor of some of its members marching in the funeral procession for Lincoln. Seen here is a photograph of Lincoln shortly before his death, but it is not the photograph that Solomons allegedly took.

Hester Street,
New York.

The Lower East Side of New York City was home to many Jews before they migrated south to Washington, D.C. Morris and Annie Garfinkle were typical of Lower East Side people; they lived on Bayard Street in a tenement house prior to moving to Washington, D.C. It is estimated that more than 40 percent of Jews who migrated to Washington, D.C., came from New York City.

12

One

PRAYING TOGETHER

That I dwell in the house of the Lord all the days of my life.

—Psalms

When the Holy Temple was destroyed in Jerusalem two millennia ago, the Jews were dispersed around the globe with a majority of Jews settling in what is now the European continent. The Jews were able to survive and not perish since they banded together for protection against a hostile world. This became fertile ground for economic isolation and discrimination that resulted in terrible pogroms. It was the synagogue that became the glue that held the Jews together and maintained their identity.

It is no wonder that when the Jews migrated to Washington, D.C., the first order of business was to establish the synagogue, which would become the organizing force in their life. The first synagogue was established in April 1852 at the home of H. Lisberger on Pennsylvania Avenue near Twenty-first Street. It later became known as the Washington Hebrew Congregation. By 1854, its membership grew to about 40 individuals.

Though Washington, D.C., had legal provisions for land to be used for building churches, there were no provisions in existence for land use to build a synagogue. In 1856, a bill was passed that allowed for the establishment of a synagogue in Washington, D.C. It was referred to in Congress as "An act for the benefit of the Hebrew Congregation in the City of Washington." On June 2, 1856, Pres. Franklin Pierce signed off on this bill, making it legal to build a synagogue in Washington, D.C. It is important to note that the first synagogue in Washington, D.C., the Washington Hebrew Congregation, was Orthodox and later aligned themselves with the Reform movement.

The second synagogue to be organized in Washington, D.C., was Adas Israel Synagogue in 1869, followed by Ohev Shalom in 1886, Talmud Torah in 1889 (which merged with Ohev Shalom in 1960), Voliner Anshe Sefard in 1907 (which merged with Har Zion in 1917 to become what is now known as Beth Shalom), Tifereth Israel in 1907, and Kesher Israel in 1910. By 1960, there were no fewer than 25 synagogues in the Washington metropolitan area.

13

The building of the Washington Hebrew Congregation stood on Eighth Street between H and I Streets and was dedicated in 1898. President McKinley, who attended the cornerstone laying one year earlier, sent his regrets that he could not attend the dedication ceremony of the new building. Currently it is the home of the New Hope Baptist Church. (Courtesy of New Hope Baptist Church; photograph by Limor Garfinkle.)

The interior of the synagogue, although changed to meet the needs of the current church, still has some of the original look of the old Washington Hebrew Congregation synagogue. Notice the menorah where the Torah scrolls used to be kept. (Courtesy of New Hope Baptist Church; photograph by Limor Garfinkle.)

It is noteworthy that the Washington Hebrew Congregation maintains an excellent relationship with the New Hope Baptist Church to this day. Occasionally, there are joint programs shared together by the church and the Washington Hebrew Congregation. (Courtesy of New Hope Baptist Church; photograph by Limor Garfinkle.)

The rear of the New Hope Baptist Church still displays the Star of David. The church takes pride in the Jewish symbols that still adorn the building. (Courtesy of New Hope Baptist Church; photograph by Limor Garfinkle.)

In 1869, the Washington Hebrew Congregation installed an organ in the synagogue, which is not permitted for use on the Sabbath and major festivals according to strict Jewish law. Other reforms were made, such as eliminating certain prayers from the service. These acts caused 35 members to break away from Washington Hebrew and establish the Adas Israel Congregation. The split was very cordial, and Washington Hebrew let Adas Israel borrow a Torah scroll until they were able to afford one of their own. Pictured here is the first Adas Israel Synagogue on Sixth and G Streets. (Courtesy of the Jewish Historical Society of Greater Washington.)

Pres. Ulysses S. Grant and his cabinet attended the dedication of the Adas Israel building. Pictured is the building in its present location. The sale of this building in 1905 fetched $14,000. (Courtesy of the Jewish Historical Society of Greater Washington.)

The first Adas Israel Synagogue, before its move to its present location at Third and G Streets, is shown here. The building was a carry-out deli prior to the move. (Courtesy of the Jewish Historical Society of Greater Washington.)

Adas Israel is the only synagogue in the United States that was preserved by actually moving the building to another location to save it from being razed. Adas Israel Synagogue moved from Sixth and G Streets to its current home at Third and G Streets in 1969. (Courtesy of the Jewish Historical Society of Greater Washington.)

Adas Israel moved to Sixth and I Streets in 1908, and the synagogue remained there for the next 43 years. In 1910, Adas Israel went from an Orthodox to becoming a Conservative synagogue. The old Adas Israel has been restored to its original grandeur and has been renamed the Historic Sixth and I Street Synagogue. (Photograph by Limor Garfinkle.)

Looking upward, viewers can appreciate the heavenly beauty of this synagogue with its stained-glass windows. (Photograph by Limor Garfinkle.)

Adas Israel moved to its present location in 1951 to a magnificent structure that stands proud until this day. It is one of the few synagogues that does not have any current plans to move its facilities to the suburbs of Maryland or Virginia. Keep in mind that the Washington Hebrew Congregation has an off branch located in Potomac, Maryland. Beth Shalom moved its entire facility to Potomac, and Ohev Shalom has an off branch in Olney, Maryland. Adas Israel is currently located at Connecticut Avenue and Porter Street NW and is thriving. (Photograph by Limor Garfinkle.)

The sanctuary at Adas Israel is quite large and magnificent. Ironically, the synagogue has an organ in the main sanctuary that is used for Saturday services, which is against Jewish law. (Photograph by Limor Garfinkle.)

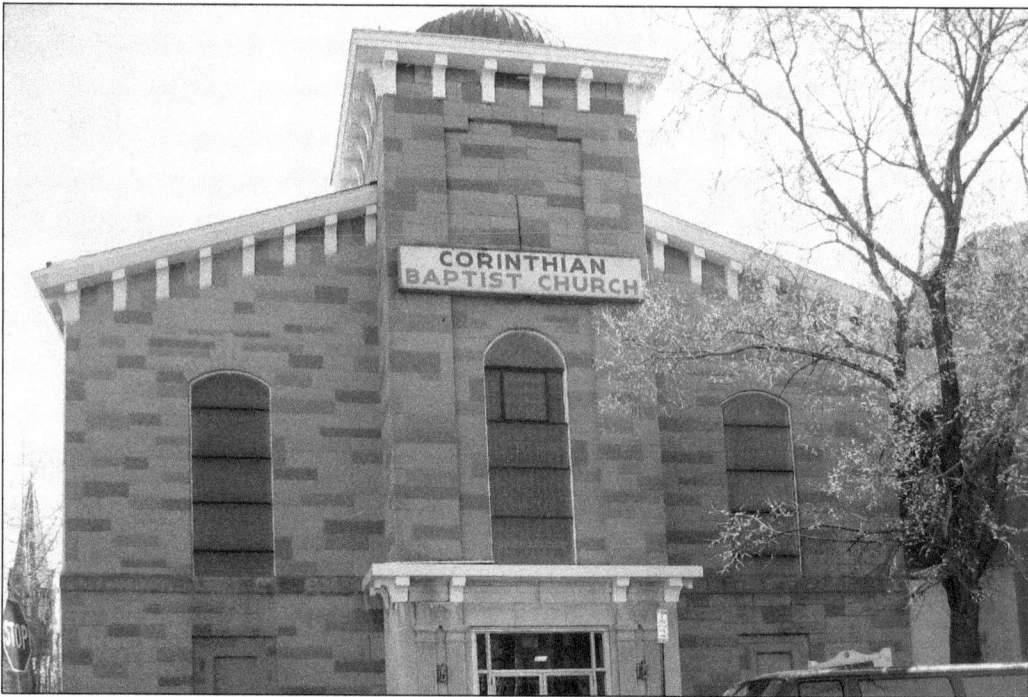

The oldest Orthodox synagogue in Washington, D.C., today is the Ohev Shalom Talmud Torah Congregation, which was established in 1869. Its first building was at Fifth and I Streets NW. The Corinthian Baptist Church is currently occupying it. (Photograph by Limor Garfinkle.)

In 1959, the oldest Southwest synagogue, Talmud Torah, merged with Ohev Shalom to become one entity known today as Ohev Shalom Talmud Torah Congregation. Pictured here is the old Talmud Torah Synagogue at 467 East Street SW, which was demolished in 1959. Rabbi Moses Yoelson, whose son was the legendary Al Jolson, was the rabbi of this synagogue for a period of time during the earlier part of the 20th century. (Courtesy of Ohev Shalom Talmud Torah Congregation.)

Talmud Torah was demolished and razed in 1958. There are no traces left of the old building as magnificent as it was. (Courtesy of the Jewish Historical Society of Greater Washington.)

Pictured here is the second location of Talmud Torah, which was purchased in 1953 from Bnai Israel; it was located at Fourteenth and Emerson Streets NW until the late 1950s.

For one year, the combined synagogue assembled for prayer at the Hebrew Academy of Washington on Sixteenth Street until the current building was opened in 1960. Pictured here is the current Ohev Shalom Synagogue located at Sixteenth and Jonquil Streets NW. (Photograph by Limor Garfinkle.)

This is the main sanctuary of Ohev Shalom Talmud Torah as it looks today. It has not been changed or remolded since its opening in 1960. Rabbi Shmuel Herzfeld, the current rabbi, has moved his seat off of the bima (platform) to make it more people friendly, as can be seen from this picture. (Photograph by Limor Garfinkle.)

There are only two synagogues in the Washington, D.C., area that are located directly across the street from one another. Pictured here is the Tifereth Israel Congregation, which was founded in 1907 as an Orthodox synagogue and is across the street from Ohev Shalom. It presently is a Conservative synagogue and has been in its current building since the late 1950s. (Photograph by Limor Garfinkle.)

A public installation of officers took place at the first Ohev Shalom at Fifth and I Streets NW in 1918. This was the first documented photograph of such an event taking place. This is a life-size image that is currently located on the back wall of the memorabilia room at Ohev Shalom Talmud Torah, located on Sixteenth Street NW. (Courtesy of Ohev Shalom Talmud Torah Congregation.)

This is the presentation of the American and Jewish flags to the congregation of Talmud Torah by the Morgenstein and Munitz families on September 28, 1948. The presentation of both an American flag and Israeli flag together celebrated the recent statehood of Israel, which took place four months prior. It was also symbolic of the strong ties between the United Sates and the new State of Israel. (Courtesy of Ohev Shalom Talmud Torah Congregation.)

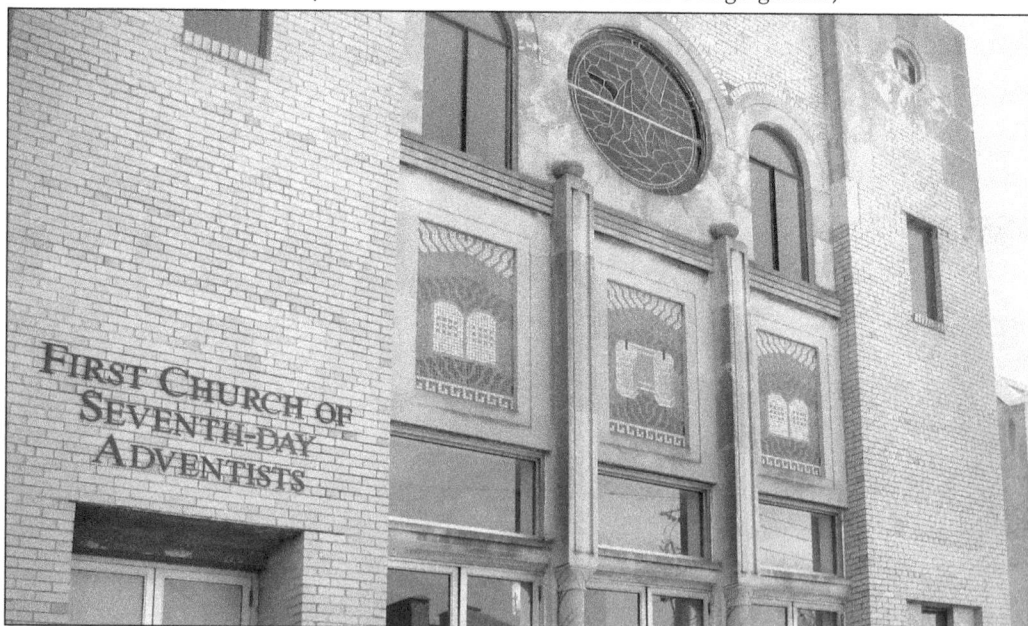

Beth Shalom is the second-oldest Orthodox synagogue in Washington D.C., having been organized first as the Har Zion Synagogue and later combined with the.Voliner Anshe Sefard. Beth Shalom built a magnificent synagogue in the late 1930s at Eighth and Shepherd Streets. Its original structure is still standing and is well maintained by the church that now occupies it. There has been very little change to the original building. (Photograph by Limor Garfinkle.)

24

This confirmation took place at Beth Shalom in the main sanctuary when it was located at Eighth and Shepherd Streets during the late 1940s or early 1950s. Confirmations celebrated the educational achievement of young Jewish girls. The notion of a bat mitzvah was foreign until recent years. (Courtesy of Beth Shalom.)

This is the sanctuary of the old Beth Shalom Congregation, which is now the main sanctuary of the church, as it looked in May 2005. The men and women used to sit separately with the women sitting upstairs on the balcony. The women's balcony is clearly visible in this picture. Beth Shalom moved to Thirteenth and Eastern Streets in 1958. (Courtesy of Beth Shalom; photograph by Limor Garfinkle.)

This May 2005 photograph shows the exterior of Beth Shalom at Thirteenth and Eastern Streets. Virtually no changes have been made to the external structure of this building since it was built in 1958. (Photograph by Limor Garfinkle.)

Pictured here is the exterior of Beth Shalom in 2005 facing the opposite side of Eastern Avenue. (Photograph by Limor Garfinkle.)

The main sanctuary at Thirteenth Street and Eastern Avenue was truly magnificent. No synagogue approaches its beauty to this day. In this picture, a wedding ceremony was taking place. (Courtesy of Beth Shalom.)

This is a closer view of this magnificent sanctuary. The ark was surrounded by pure-white polished marble. Legend has it that the marble used to construct the setting around the ark came from Israel. Beth Shalom is now located in Potomac, Maryland. (Courtesy of Beth Shalom.)

ANNOUNCEMENT

Realizing the great need for a Synagogue for this locality, the HAR ZION CONGREGATION of Georgia Avenue, Petworth and Vicinity, announce the purchase of the beautiful three story building located on the S. E. Cor. Georgia Ave. and Randolph St. modern and up-to-date in every respect, from which we hope to make as fine a Synagogue as can be found anywhere in the District of Columbia. If we get the support of every Jew who is interested in this great undertaking, it can be realized. We want your moral aid especially and your financial support if you can give it. We cordially invite you to observe the Passover Services in this new building.

PROMINENT SPEAKERS WILL ADDRESS YOU AND EXPLAIN OUR PURPOSE TO YOU. BE SURE TO ATTEND AND BRING YOUR FRIENDS WITH YOU. LET'S GET TO-GETHER AND WORK.

WE MUST HAVE A SYNAGOGUE, and with your help WE SHALL HAVE IT.

Respectfully,

ABRAHAM FISHBEIN,
Secretary.

The Hanford Press, 810 F St. N. W.

This announcement was posted on the street by members of Har Zion before it was incorporated into the Beth Shalom Congregation. The sign, geared toward gaining new members and raising money to build a new synagogue, was probably posted in the mid- to late 1920s. (Courtesy of Beth Shalom.)

Kesher Israel was organized in 1910 and is the only Orthodox synagogue located in the heart of Georgetown. This is the original synagogue building before it was torn down and refurbished during the early 1930s. (Courtesy of Kesher Israel.)

The groundbreaking ceremony at Kesher Israel occurred during the late 1920s or early 1930. There have been no changes made to the building since the 1930s with the exception of the cornerstone being raised from the lower part of the building to shoulder level. (Courtesy of Kesher Israel.)

In this picture of the groundbreaking ceremony at Kesher Israel c. 1929 or 1930, one can notice the patriotism of the congregates. Kesher Israel is located less than two miles from the White House. (Courtesy of Kesher Israel.)

This is the dedication of the Kesher Israel building in 1931. The man standing on the left side with his hand on the wall is Morris Garfinkle. (Courtesy of Adam Garfinkle.)

The Kesher Israel Synagogue is shown here as it looks today. Notice the cornerstone on the right, which indicates that the synagogue was organized in 1911 and rebuilt in 1931. (Photograph by Limor Garfinkle.)

Mrs. Harris (Fannie) Levy was the first ladies' auxiliary president of the Kesher Israel Synagogue in 1911. What is remarkable is that Kesher Israel is an Orthodox synagogue where women would be encouraged to be involved with their families and not the demands of synagogue leadership. (Courtesy of Kesher Israel.)

This portrait of an unidentified bar mitzvah boy was found in the archives of Kesher Israel. What is striking about this picture is the formality of the boy in his robe and old-fashioned skullcap. The picture was probably taken in the 1920s or 1930s. (Courtesy of Kesher Israel.)

Two

MAKING A LIVING

You open up your hand and satisfy the desire of every living thing.

—Psalms

The Jews of Washington, D.C., did not initially come to the nation's capital to seek out government jobs. Most of the Jews who made their life in Washington, D.C., at the turn of the early 20th century were looking for economic opportunity to provide for their families. At some later point during the century, Jews did find opportunity within the government.

Harry Berger came to Washington, D.C., from Poland during the mid-1930s when the Jewish community of Washington, D.C., was growing. As was typical of Jews who wanted to leave their mother country, he went to his rabbi to discuss the matter. Upon agreeing to keep the commandments of the Torah and to resist "Americanization" since the United States was considered *treif* (non-kosher), Berger emigrated to escape from the hardships of life. Many who preceded Berger gave up religion in exchange for economic opportunity.

Upon arriving in America, Berger settled in Williamsburg, Brooklyn. Although relatives took him in and cared for him, he was quickly discouraged by Jewish life in the United States. Sweatshops abounded. Conditions were harsh and unsafe as was learned from the tragic Triangle Fire in New York on Saturday, March 11, 1911, which killed many young Jewish women.

Berger decided to be a peddler, but many New York peddlers could not provide for their families. So individuals like Berger traveled from city to city to peddle their goods and returned before the Sabbath. Berger traveled to Boston where opportunity was fair, but after a year, he realized that he could not make a good living there.

He then traveled to Washington, D.C., and fell in love with the Washington Jewish community. He peddled briefly while he put enough money away to purchase a building that became a small clothing store, simply called "Berger's."

Jews owned numerous gas stations in Washington, D.C. Paul Himmelfarb came to Washington, D.C., in 1915. His network of filling stations for oil and kerosene for household purposes grew. He had a keen eye for business, realizing that the automobile had a thirst for gasoline. In 1930, the well-known Amoco/Standard Oil Company leased his filing stations. Pulling in to this gas station during the late 1930s or 1940s for a fill-up would have cost you only pennies a gallon.

Washington Jews were active in the automobile accessory field. This automobile accident occurred in Washington, D.C., and might have necessitated parts from a Jewish automobile accessory merchant.

Washington Jews during the 1920s and beyond became automobile retailers. Washingtonians are familiar with the names of Ourisman and Lustine Chevrolet, Blank Pontiac, Cherner Ford, and Herson Foreign Auto. The Washington Cadillac Company, seen here c. 1930s, was probably not owned by Hews; however, it is said that Morris Cafritz, a Jewish philanthropist, was particular about the cars he drove and preferred the Cadillac. In all probability he purchased his Caddy from the Washington Cadillac Company, since it was the only show in town for numerous years.

This famous corner was known as "the busy corner" on Eighth Street and Market Space. S. Kann Sons was owned by Jews; it was well known simply as Kann's Department Store. Seen here is the store during the 1920s.

In this picture of a Washington, D.C., shopping area during the late 1920s is a store owned by a man whose last name was Notes (to the left). Notes was an unusual name that was Americanized from the longer version of Notesky, Notestein, or Notesberg. Quite common in those days was for Jews to either radically change their name or "Americanize" it to hide their Jewish identity.

Harry Berger owned a small clothing store at 3411 Georgia Avenue NW. As was common with many small Jewish business owners, the Bergers' house was located behind the storefront. Berger lived with his family behind the store until they moved farther uptown in 1958.

Wolf and Anna Weiner are seen here in the early 1920s. Since the owner's store and house were closely intertwined, many visitors would stop by to chat. The Weiners were regular visitors to the Bergers when they owned the store at 3411 Georgia Avenue NW. They often visited for hours at a time.

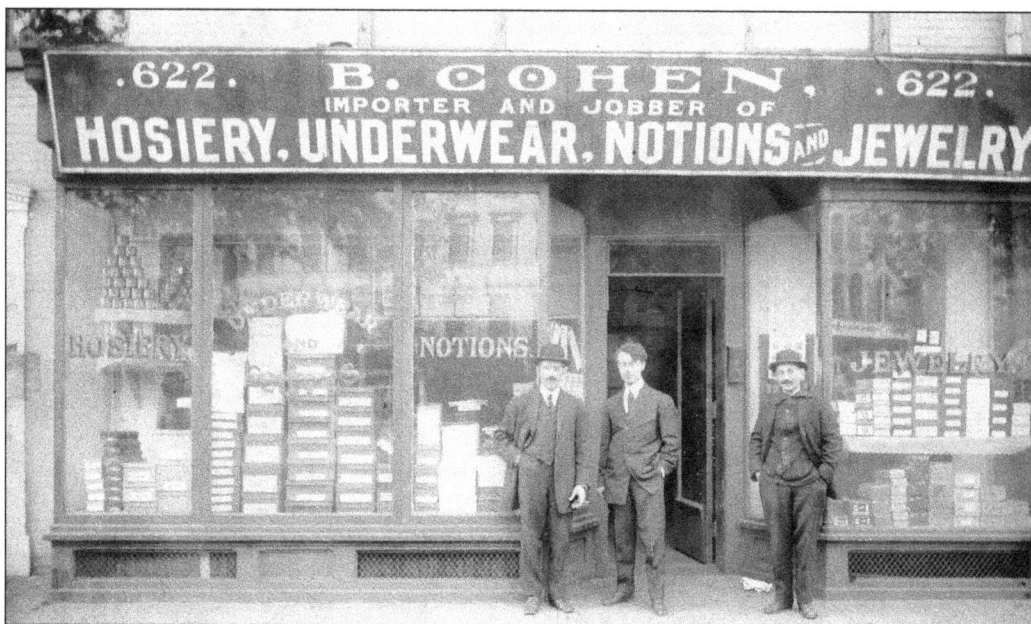

Cohen's clothing and jewelry store in Washington, D.C. was not an unusual mixture of how Jews who owned small businesses made a living to survive. If a women purchased a new dress, then ultimately she could be persuaded to buy a new piece of jewelry to make the dress look more attractive. (Courtesy of the Jewish Historical Society of Greater Washington.)

The DGS store, shown here c. 1921, was a consortium of 12 Jewish grocers who formed a cooperative in order to boost their buying power and attract a wider net of customers. If customers could afford to pay $2,500 as an initiation fee, which was quite expensive in those days, they could obtain goods at cost. (Courtesy of the Jewish Historical Society of Washington.)

The Economy Meat Market in Washington, D.C., is seen here. Most Jews who sold meat were kosher in those days. It was not unusual for women to go to the butcher on Thursday and pick out a live chicken to be ritually slaughtered by a rabbi or a ritual slaughterer (shochet). Once the chicken was killed, the butcher would pluck its feathers, drain the blood, and soak it in salt for a prescribed period of time. This would render the chicken kosher. Many Jewish women, to save a few dollars a month, would pluck the feathers and soak and salt the meat themselves. (Courtesy of the Jewish Historical Society of Washington.)

Jews owned jewelry stores such as Castleberg's and Hochberg's, which is seen here. However, the jewelry business, as well as pawn shops, was not a popular business for Washington, D.C., Jews since they would be competing against well-known department stores that sold jewelry such as the Hecht and Company and Lansburghs Department Stores (owned by Jews). (Courtesy of the Jewish Historical Society of Washington.)

Above left: Joseph Fenster owned the New York Bakery for many years before it was sold and went out of business. Fenster baked bread fresh on a daily basis. Many Washington Jews went there to buy challah before the Sabbath and bagels on Sunday. Pictured here is Joe Fenster baking bread at the New York Bakery. (Courtesy of Dr. Harvey Fenster.)

Above right: This sticker was attached to each bread that was baked at New York Bakery. Many stores that were owned by Jews were located on the Georgia Avenue strip. (Courtesy of Dr. Harvey Fenster.)

The Klivitskys owned a store called Klivitsky's, which was a kosher meat and grocery store. They sold baked goods as well as fresh bread. Bob Klivitsky shortened and Americanized his name to Klevits. Shown here are Bob's parents in front of the shop, located at 1702 Seventh Street NW, in 1918. (Courtesy of Ohev Shalom Talmud Torah Congregation.)

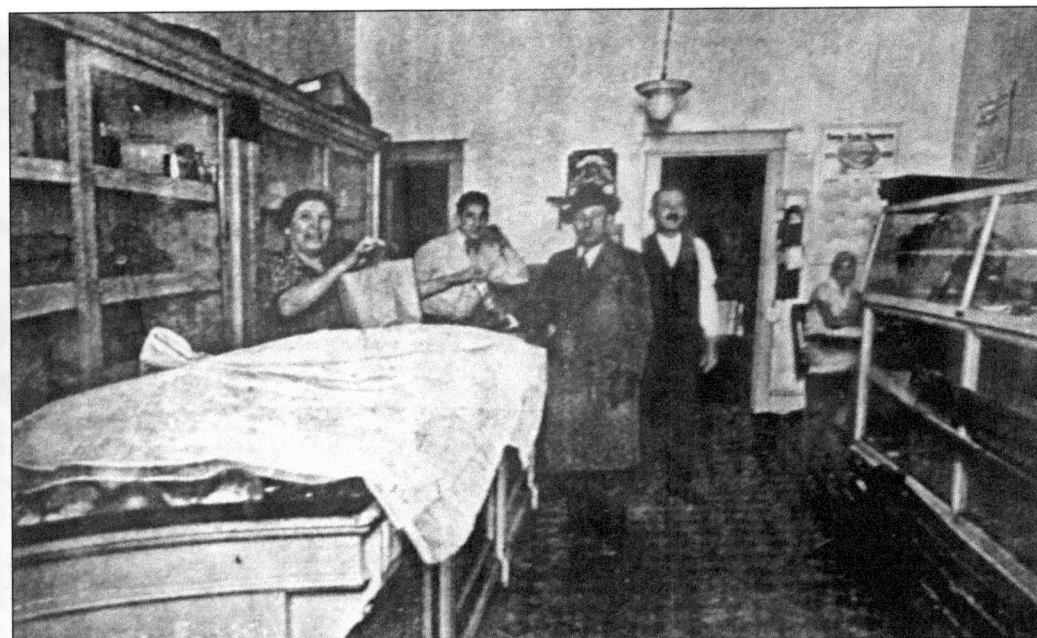

This is the Morgenstein's bakery, c. 1918. Jews frequently owned stores that sold food since food was a necessity of life that could earn a decent living for the proprietor. (Courtesy of Ohev Shalom Talmud Torah Congregation.)

A very unusual business owned by Jews, the Dime Messenger Service is pictured here in 1912. It was probably called the Dime since that was the cost of delivering a message in those years. In front are the young messengers on bicycle. (Courtesy of the Jewish Historical Society of Washington.)

The Shankmans are seen here in their small grocery store, *c.* 1918. They sold both kosher and non-kosher goods. (Courtesy of the Jewish Historical Society of Greater Washington.)

The Kronheim Lunchroom was famous for who it attracted. Judge Milton Kronheim was instrumental in getting President Truman to break ground at the new Washington Hebrew Congregation on Macomb Avenue. Pictured clockwise from left center are Supreme Court Justice Arthur Goldberg (on phone), Sen. Abe Ribicoff, land developer Charles E. Smith, Judge David Bazelon, unidentified, Arnold Shaw, sportswriter Morrie Siegel, Judge J. Skelly Wright, unidentified, and Milton Kronheim. Judge Kronheim's father was one of the largest liquor distributors to liquor stores in the Washington, D.C., area. (Courtesy of the Jewish Historical Society of Greater Washington.)

It was estimated that by 1960, 75 percent of all liquor stores in Washington, D.C., were owned by Jewish merchants. Liquor stores in those days were not consumed by chain stores. If you could obtain a license to sell liquor, you could make a nice living. Pictured here is a liquor store in Washington, D.C., during the World War II years.

Cathedral Liquors was located directly across the street from the Washington National Zoo. The owner was Howard S. Garfinkle, who died while working in the store in April 1987.

Pictured here are Harry and Jenny Berger when they first moved to Washington D.C., c. 1936. (Courtesy of Sidney Berger.)

There was one Jewish bookstore in Washington, D.C., until the 1960s, the Kennedy Street Hebrew Book Store, located on Kennedy Street NW. Now there are two Jewish bookstores located in Wheaton, Maryland. Miriam Lisbon is pictured here in Lisbon's Hebrew Books and Gifts, next to Shalom Strictly Kosher Market. (Photograph by Limor Garfinkle.)

The second bookstore, the Jewish Book Store of Greater Washington, is located several blocks away from the first bookstore. Standing by the Torah scroll is Menachem Youlus, who is the owner. The Torah in the picture is being donated to the Ethiopian Jewish community in Beit Shemesh, Israel. (Photograph by Limor Garfinkle.)

MEET YOUR FRIENDS AT

HOFBERG'S

The place to go for the
finest in
Kosher Delicatessen Food

7822 Eastern Ave. N.W.
(corner of Georgia and Eastern Aves.)

AMPLE PARKING IN REAR

Open 'til 2 A.M.   RA. 3-5878

Although there were a few kosher restaurants, primarily located in Georgetown, during the early part of 20th century, few endured as a legend. Hofberg's, located at Eastern Avenue, opened in the 1930s and was still in existence in the 1980s. This advertisement for Hofberg's is dated to 1959. Although Hofberg's was advertised as kosher, it was more aptly described as kosher-style.

בשר כשר

Posin's

Super Market

One of Washington's
Great Stores
Since 1860

LANSBURGH'S
7th, 8th and E Streets
NAtional 9800

Above left: Every Washington Jew was familiar with this logo, since this kosher delicatessen and bakery spanned over four decades on Georgia Avenue.

Above right: Landsburgh's Department Store was the first department store to open in Washington that was owned by Jews. It opened in 1860 and advertised frequently, as with this advertisement from the 1920s.

וַיֶּעֱשׂוּ לִי מִקְדָּשׁ
וְשָׁכַנְתִּי בְּתוֹכָם.

" AND LET THEM MAKE
ME A SANCTUARY: THAT
I MAY DWELL AMONG THEM "

The inscription on the outside wall of Ohev Shalom Talmud Torah Congregation stands out boldly and can be read easily from the cars traveling north or south on Sixteenth Street since 1960. (Photograph by Limor Garfinkle.)

Old-time Washington, D.C., Jews will associate the funeral business with the name Bernard Danzansky. Danzansky was the first Jewish funeral home to open in Washington, D.C., in 1912. The Danzansky funeral home still serves the Jewish population, although other Jewish funeral homes exist in the area. This is a funeral hearse, c. 1925.

Kornhauser Grocery Store, here *c.* 1910, was owned by German Jews. It is important to note that the early Washington Jews before 1910 were overwhelmingly but not exclusively of German extraction, and hence many of the early stores owned by Jews had Germanic names. (Courtesy of the Jewish Historical Society of Greater Washington.)

Pictured here is Harvey's Famous Restaurant on Connecticut Avenue. Although this was not a kosher establishment, it was well known for its fish dinners. Jews who were not strictly kosher would eat here, and Jewish organizations would book affairs to be held at Harvey's.

Shalom Strictly Kosher Market is located next to Max's, a strictly kosher restaurant unique for offering American, Chinese, and Israeli cuisine together. The market offers a large selection of kosher food including fresh baked goods. (Photograph by Limor Garfinkle.)

Most of the kosher supermarkets and restaurants serving the Jewish community of Washington are located in nearby suburban Maryland. Pictured here is Max's, which was opened in the late 1980s and has a large menu of selections from Israeli to Chinese cuisine. (Photograph by Limor Garfinkle.)

Three

THE PEOPLE AND ITS INSTITUTIONS

If I am not for myself who will be for me? If I am only for myself what am I?

—*Ethics of the Fathers*

As the Jewish community grew, there arose a need for institutions that would meet the needs of children, families, and the elderly. From the early 20th century and beyond, the Jewish community of Washington, D.C., established a Jewish Community Center, Hebrew Home for the Aged, the Chevra Kadisha Society to attend to the ritual needs of the deceased, and a community-sponsored Hebrew school to educate the children, to name just a few. As these institutions became viable and grew in size, the Jewish community became stronger and attracted more Jews to the area.

The synagogues of Washington, D.C., continued to develop and extend their reach to meet many of the social needs of the Jews. Washington Jews were an interesting and a diverse group of individuals.

Seen here is the Young Man's Hebrew Association (YMHA) bulletin of 1917. In those days, the YMHA's facilities were used by other Jewish organizations, such as synagogues. The YMHA provided activities for all ages and was a precursor to the Jewish Community Center of Greater Washington. (Courtesy of the Jewish Historical Society of Greater Washington D.C.)

By the 1920s, it became obvious that a Jewish Community Center was needed because the YWHA quarters were not adequate to meet the needs of a rapidly growing Jewish community. Groundbreaking for the new Jewish Community Center took place on May 3, 1925. The center would eventually become the meeting place for no less than six Jewish organizations, such as Bnai Brith, Hadassah, and the American Jewish Committee. (Courtesy of Phyllis Lincoln.)

The Jewish Community Center (JCC) was moved to Rockville, Maryland, during the late 1960s. The building on Sixteenth Street was eventually sold. In an unprecedented move, the building was repurchased during the 1990s to accommodate the rebirth of the growing Washington Jewish community. (Photograph by Limor Garfinkle.)

Pictured here is the JCC basketball team standing outside of the building in 1932. Irving Tash is in the back row far left. This team played in the city athletic league against the YMCA in Washington, D.C. The JCC were the athletic league champions in 1930 and 1931. (Courtesy of the Jewish Historical Society of Greater Washington.)

The JCC basketball team in the 1950s is pictured inside the Jewish Community Center. Jerry ? and Ben ? were the coaches. The players are unidentified. (Courtesy of the Jewish Community Center.)

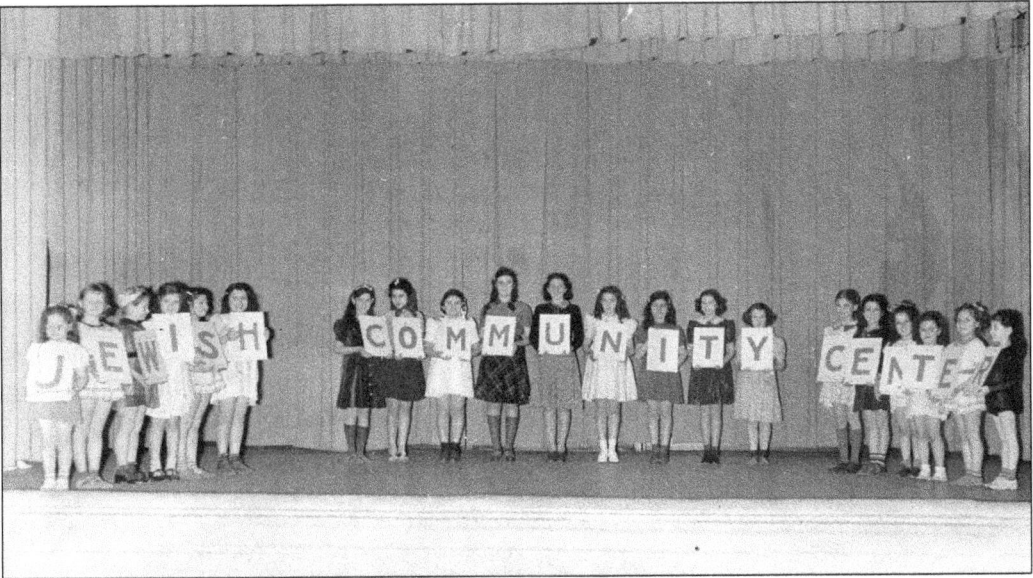

Pictured here is a girls' activity group at the Jewish Community Center. The girls in this picture range in age from 6 to 13. At times, they would put on plays for parents and would proudly display that they were part of the JCC of Washington, D.C. (Courtesy of the Jewish Historical Society of Greater Washington.)

Two unidentified Jewish lovelies in Washington, D.C., stand together in this c. 1920s picture. They were members of the Jewish Community Center. (Courtesy of the Jewish Historical Society of Greater Washington.)

A Washington, D.C., bathing suit beauties contest is shown here. The two cup holders were Jewish. Second from left is Anna Neibel, and next to her is Eva Fridell around the 1920s.

Jewish children stand on the steps of the Jewish Community Center at a day camp. This was an important service for parents who needed to provide structure for their kids, and it provided the Jewish Community Center with the opportunity to fulfill an important need to Jewish children who were not affiliated with a synagogue. (Courtesy of the Jewish Historical Society of Greater Washington.)

Pictured here is a *c.* 1940 dinner to raise money for the Hebrew Home for the Aged. Morris Garfinkle, one of the founders of the Hebrew Home for the Aged, is seated at the right. (Courtesy of Phyllis Lincoln.)

The Washington Jewish community as a whole was a strong supporter of Palestine. In the 1920s, Palestine was considered a British mandate. Shown here are D.C. Zionists and their meeting with the British Envoy on April 1, 1925. (Courtesy of Phyllis Lincoln.)

Adolphus S. Solomons was a prominent Washington Jew who befriended Pres. Abraham Lincoln. The portrait of him seen here was probably taken at his Washington, D.C., photographic studio located at 911 Pennsylvania Avenue. Solomons's greatest accomplishment was in the service of the Red Cross. Solomons assisted Clara Barton with the establishment of the Red Cross in 1881. (Courtesy of the American Jewish Historical Society.)

Pictured here is a branch of the Red Cross that consisted exclusively of Jewish women. This picture was taken during World War II, and these women were volunteers at a time when their service was desperately needed. Many worked at Walter Reed Army Hospital in Washington. (Courtesy of Sidney Berger.)

For teenage males, Bnai Brith sponsored several AZA youth groups. AZA stands for the American Zionist Association. The young men here are members of the Wilner AZA group during the 1940s. (Courtesy of Sidney Berger.)

Simon Atlas AZA was a popular male fraternity sponsored by Washington, D.C.'s Bnai Brith. Many Jewish males joined AZA for its spectacular social events. Young women would join BBG, which stood for Bnai Brith Girls. Notice the formal dress of these young men. This c. 1940 picture in all probability was taken before the annual dance prior to summer vacation. The young ladies were probably waiting for their gents in another room. (Courtesy of Erwin Garfinkle.)

This is the annual banquet of the social club of the Hebrew Home for the Aged that took place at Harvey's Restaurant on May 1, 1927. This picture is a complete mystery because young adults and not senior citizens are seated around the table. Is it possible that in order to raise money, the Hebrew Home for the Aged sponsored a club for singles?

The proper ritual cleansing for the deceased in preparation for burial was the responsibility of the Chevra Kadisha. This picture was taken at their annual meeting in 1928 at a private home. The participants of this Chevra Kadisha were members of Talmud Torah Congregation, which later merged with Ohev Shalom. Morris Garfinkle is sitting at the left with his arm resting on the table. The bearded man sitting at the back of the room is Rabbi Moses Aaron Horwitz. Rabbi Horwitz was a Talmudic scholar and the spiritual leader of Talmud Torah until his death in 1935. He replaced the Rabbi Moses Yoelson as spiritual leader of Talmud Torah in 1912. It was said of him that "he was loved and respected by all of Washington Jewry."

The meeting of the Chevra Kadisha Talmud Torah Congregation is taking place here c. 1937. (Courtesy of Ohev Shalom Talmud Torah Congregation.)

The national conference of the Union of Orthodox Congregations in 1935 took place at the JCC on Sixteenth Street. In attendance that day and pictured in the front row were Rabbis Gedalia Silverstone, Dr. Julius T. Loeb, and Zemach Green, Cantor ? Novick, Bernard Danzansky, and the president of Yeshiva University, Rabbi Dr. Samuel Belkin. (Courtesy of Ohev Shalom Talmud Torah Congregation.)

Pictured here is an unidentified Jewish cadet in Washington, D.C. The Jews of Washington, D.C., had their own Jewish Cadet Corps so there was no meeting or drills on the holy Sabbath. Non-Jewish units would drill and meet on Saturday, which was not permitted by Jewish law. Some drills actually took place at Griffith Stadium where the Washington Senators used to play. (Courtesy of the Jewish Historical Society of Greater Washington.)

This dinner, which took place in 1936, was held in honor of the esteemed Rabbi Gedalia Silverstone. Rabbi Silverstone came to Washington, D.C., in 1906 and served as the first rabbi of the Ohev Shalom Synagogue, located at Fifth and I Streets NW. He left Washington, D.C., in the 1920s to settle in Palestine but returned in the 1930s to become the rabbi of Tifereth Israel Synagogue when it was located at Fourteenth and Euclid Streets NW. He went back to Israel after the country proclaimed its independence in 1948. Pictured from left to right are Rabbis Jacob Dubrow, Gedalia Silverstone, and Samuel Klavan in prayer on April 20, 1936. (Courtesy of Ohev Shalom Talmud Torah Congregation.)

This Passover seder took place in April 1928. Morris Garfinkle had 10 children and numerous

grandchildren. Morris Garfinkle is on the far right, and his wife, Annie, is sitting next to him.

This confirmation class was at Bnai Israel at Fourteenth and Emerson Streets, c. 1920. Confirmation was popular for women, unlike men who had the bar mitzvah at the age of 13 as prescribed by Jewish custom. Women were confirmed at the age of 16 to encourage further Jewish education beyond the age of 13. (Courtesy of the Jewish Historical Society of Greater Washington.)

Pictured here is an Adas Israel confirmation at Sixth and I Streets. (Courtesy of the Jewish Historical Society of Greater Washington.)

The children's choir at Ezras Israel is pictured here c. 1930. (Courtesy of the Jewish Historical Society of Greater Washington.)

Pictured here is the Adas Israel Choir, c. 1920s. (Courtesy of the Jewish Historical Society of Greater Washington.)

Prior to the 1970s, most girls were confirmed and did not participate in a bat mitzvah ceremony. Confirmation was an indication that a young woman had attended Hebrew school. This is a confirmation class at Beth Shalom Congregation, c. 1950. (Courtesy of Beth Shalom.)

Cantor Shalom Katz of the Beth Shalom Synagogue is blessing a bar mitzvah boy during a candle-lighting ceremony, c. 1950. (Courtesy of Beth Shalom.)

Shalom Katz was a world-renowned cantor whose melodious soprano voice was a legend at Beth Shalom. Later he became the cantor for Tifereth Israel Synagogue. Legend has it that Cantor Katz was about to be killed by the Nazis during the holocaust. In anticipation of being killed by an SS man, he started to sing the Kaddish. The Nazi SS man was so overwhelmed with the beauty of his voice that the cantor's life was spared. In this picture, Cantor Katz appears to be leading the service when Beth Shalom was located at Eighth and Shepherd Streets. Wearing a white robe may indicate that he was officiating during the High Holiday season. Cantor Katz died in the 1980s, but the tapes of his golden voice are sold in Jewish bookstores throughout the country today. (Courtesy of Beth Shalom.)

A double wedding ceremony performed by Rabbi Zemach Green at Ohev Shalom Synagogue on September 2, 1934, is shown here. Harry and Rose Simon are on the left. Sophia and Ralph Friedman are on the right. Sophia is Harry's sister. Harry was bar mitzvahed at Ohev Shalom in 1920. (Courtesy of Ohev Shalom Talmud Torah Congregation.)

Morris Cafritz was one of the wealthiest Jews in Washington, D.C. He shaped the Jewish community of Washington by developing the Petworth section of Washington, D.C. There were numerous banquets and dinners dedicated to him over the years since he gave generously to several synagogues and other charitable causes. This was a testimonial dinner in memory of Nathan Cafritz on October 19, 1941. Nathan was the son of Morris Cafritz. Nathan followed in his father's footsteps and was in real estate. Like his father, he was a generous giver to Jewish institutions. (Courtesy of Ohev Shalom Talmud Torah Congregation.)

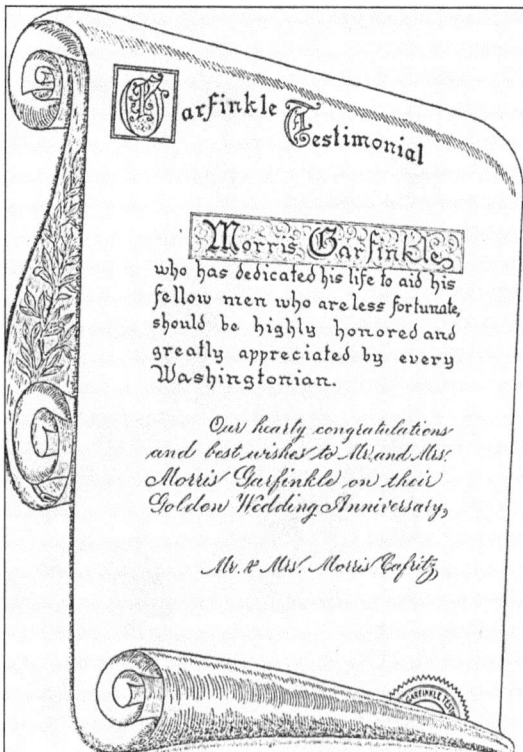

Morris Cafritz donated an entire page to the testimonial journal for Morris and Annie Garfinkle's 50th wedding anniversary dinner, c. 1943. The elaborate journal that was created for this affair was bound in leather and was done completely in calligraphy by a famous Jewish artist from Baltimore, Maryland, Samson Margolis. An example page from the book is seen here. To donate a page was quite expensive, and monies went to defray the cost of putting the journal together and to charitable causes in Washington, D.C.

Pictured here on the east side of 4 1/2 Street in the 600 block is Mary Newman (née Morganstern) with her sister and friends, c. 1918. (Courtesy of Ohev Shalom Talmud Torah Congregation.)

A distinguished and famous Jewish Washingtonian was Leopold Karpeles, who served in the army during the Civil War. He was the color bearer for his outfit, the Ninth Army Corps. He fought in a number of major battles during the War Between the States and was fortunate not to have been killed. Toward the end of the war, Gen. Ulysses S. Grant ordered his army to Richmond, and Karpeles held the colors once more. Karpeles was wounded by a Confederate bullet to the knee, but he kept going and did not drop the flag until the loss of blood sustained from his injury weakened him. Reluctantly he had to pass the American flag to another soldier in his regiment. Karpeles was sent to Washington, D.C., to recuperate. In the hospital, he met Sara, the daughter of Rabbi Mundheim, who was the spiritual leader of the Washington Hebrew Congregation. He married the rabbi's daughter, and later they produced three children. Karpeles was the first Jew to receive the Congressional Medal of Honor for his bravery. Karpeles died in 1909 and is buried in the Washington Hebrew Congregation Cemetery. (Courtesy of the Jewish Historical Society of Greater Washington.)

71

Nathan Gothelf came to the United States from Germany and was the second president of Adas Israel Congregation. He secured two Torah scrolls for the synagogue and carried the congregation through a severe economic depression that almost caused Adas Israel to become a footnote in history. Gothelf was a very learned man who easily served in numerous roles for the congregation. He was not happy with Jewish life in America and subsequently decided to return to his native home in Germany. But his dream of returning home was not to be realized; he died in 1881 from a fatal carriage accident. (Courtesy of the Jewish Historical Society of Greater Washington.)

The flag-raising at the Washington Hebrew Congregation in 1917 is taking place here. During the Great War (World War I), Jews took the opportunity to hoist the flag in support of the American troops that were fighting for our country overseas. (Courtesy of the Jewish Historical Society of Greater Washington.)

Tifereth Israel Choir is performing here during the 1950s. Most well-known synagogues in Washington, D.C., had choirs during the High Holidays of Rosh Hashanah and Yom Kippur and at other special occasions. The Orthodox synagogues only allowed men to participate in the choir, while Conservative and Reform synagogues allowed women. There was uproar in a Washington, D.C., synagogue when it became known that several members of the choir were not Jewish. (Courtesy of the Jewish Historical Society of Greater Washington.)

Pictured here is the Jewish Foster Home in Washington, D.C., c. 1920s. The Jewish Foster Home crystallized during a meeting of the Immigrant Aid Committee of the Council of Jewish Women during the early part of 1908. After World War I, the Jewish community of Washington's population was over 8,000 souls. It was a time of upheaval in Europe, but for some unaccountable reason, the number of Jewish homeless and orphaned children increased proportionately. In 1911, under the leadership of Mrs. Charles Goldsmith, money was raised to acquire property at 3213 Q Street NW, and the dwelling pictured here provided a home for many displaced Jewish children. This home was dedicated on October 29, 1911. Minnie Goldsmith worked tirelessly to make this home a reality, and she loved the orphaned and displaced kids who resided there. She was affectionately known and referred to as "Aunt" Minnie. (Courtesy of the Jewish Historical Society of Greater Washington.)

Isadore Gimble reads the Yiddish newspaper. For Yiddish-speaking, first-generation Washingtonians, reading the *Forward* was popular. Mr. Gimble was the owner of small food store called Congress. (Courtesy of the Jewish Historical Society of Greater Washington.)

Here are several rabbis and others standing in front of what appears to be the Jewish Community Center of Washington, D.C., c. 1928. On the far right in the first row is Morris Garfinkle. In the center of the third row is Rabbi Moses Yoelson, whose famous son was Al Jolson.

Mr. and Mrs. Isaac Levi and family were founders of Talmud Torah Congregation. They were owners of Levi's Busy Corner, located at 4 1/2 K Street SW. (Courtesy of the Jewish Historical Society of Greater Washington.)

Ezras Israel Synagogue was located on Eighth Street in Northeast Washington. The synagogue was founded in 1911 and endured into the 1940s. Jews from the Northeast moved to the Northwest of Washington, D.C., or into Montgomery County. Notice that the men were all wearing hats, which was a demonstration of respect for the synagogue as well as keeping up with the fashion of the times, c. 1937. (Courtesy of the Jewish Historical Society of Greater Washington.)

Four

THE CITY AND THE WASHINGTON SENATORS

For in His power are the hidden mysteries of earth and the mountain summits are His.

—Psalms

Washington, D.C., is a magnificent city. During the springtime and by early April, one can admire the cherry blossoms when standing at the Jefferson Memorial. One can wonder how many of the early Jewish settlers who came to Washington, D.C., gave much thought to the beauty of this city. Looking at old pictures of late-19th-century Washington, with Georgetown being a prime example, the city appeared dismal and unattractive. Back in those days, Georgetown was the commercial hub of the district as it was situated along the banks of the Potomac River, which separates Washington from Virginia. The famed Chesapeake and Ohio Canal started in Georgetown. Interestingly, a respectable number of the early Jews settled in or around Georgetown.

Those who grew up in Washington remember school trips to the White House, monuments, and the Capitol. Many remember going to a baseball game and watching the Washington Senators play. They were an awfully bad team with the exception of when the legendary Walter Johnson pitched the Senators to a World Series victory back in 1924. However, most Washingtonians today remember the Senators from the 1950s and 1960s when this ditty was recited, "Washington was first in war, first in peace, and last in the American league." It is not widely known that the Washington Senators had three Jewish ballplayers who were legends in their own right.

Pictured here is a tour bus in the nation's capital, c. 1915.

Jewish men of the United Lobby for Palestine (ULP) pose for a picture at the Capitol in the 1930s. (Courtesy of the Jewish Historical Society of Greater Washington.)

The Jefferson Memorial was one of the stops that Jews made while living in Washington. This was a notable spot to view the cherry blossoms in early April. Notice the cherry blossom tree in the foreground of this picture.

Here is the White House and home to our president. Many tours for Jewish schoolchildren of Washington, D.C., were conducted here.

The Washington Monument has stood proud since the day it was completed in 1885 at the cost of $1.8 million. It is the world's tallest freestanding stone structure.

Here a touring taxi standing in front of the Lincoln Memorial is ready to accept passengers for tours, c. 1920s.

This is a picture of the United States Treasury building during the 1940s. Notice the streetcars, which were used until they became outdated in the early 1960s.

Rock Creek, which flows into the Potomac River, weaves through Rock Creek Park and into Montgomery County, Maryland. If you did not own a car, you could go through the park by bus back in the 1920s.

The nation's capital has hosted many conventions of Jewish importance. Pictured here is the 46th General Assembly of the Union of Hebrew Congregations, which took place at the

Sheraton Park Hotel on November 15, 1961.

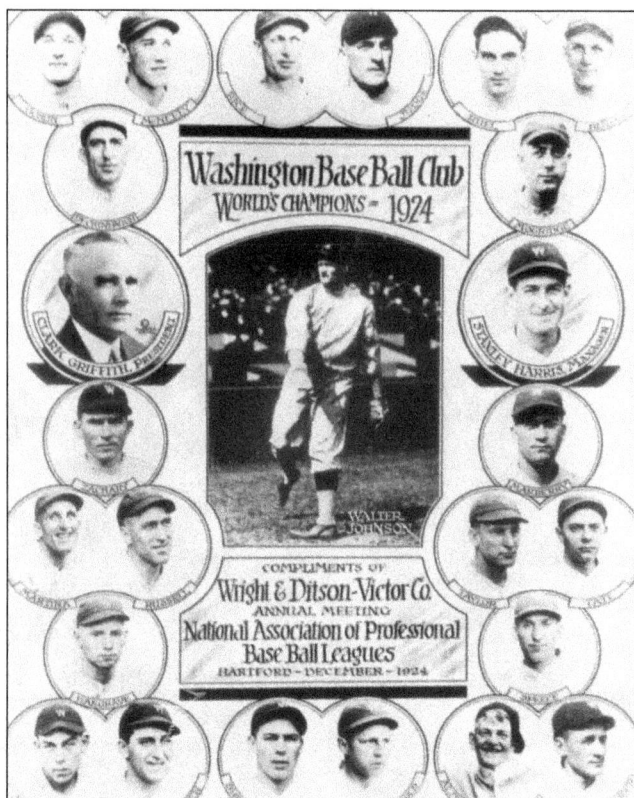

The legendary Washington Senators were World Champions in 1924. Although not too many Jewish ball players played for the Washington Senators, the few that did were notables such as Al Schacht, Buddy Meyer, and Moe Berg.

The Washington Senators struggled to play good baseball during the 1950s. WWDC was a radio station that broadcast the ball games and was popular with many Washingtonians. It still broadcasts today.

84

Al Schacht was a memorable Jewish baseball player. As legend has it, Al was asked to pitch against the Yankees. The famed Walter Johnson, the Washington Senators' best player and a baseball Hall of Famer, had just pitched a no-hitter the day prior against Boston, bruising his pitching arm. Clark Griffith, the owner and general manager of the Senators, was panic stricken since he had no pitchers capable of taking on the Yankees. Griffith told Al that if he won the game against those "damn Yanks," he would have a job as a Washington Senator for the rest of his life. Al pitched against the Yankees and won the game 4-1. Al's fame did not come from playing baseball, but for his unique personality. He was often on the ballfield dressed as a clown. His appearance drove the crowd wild, and the fans loved him. Consequently his antics were tolerated. The back of this picture reads, " 'Foul,' the umpire, yelled. Schacht responded, "and don't forget to duck." (Courtesy of the National Baseball Hall of Fame.)

Buddy Meyer played for the Washington Senators from 1925 until 1941. He was a great baseball player who almost made it into the baseball Hall of Fame. Legend has it that Meyer was traded for a player on the Boston Red Sox. Clark Griffith moaned that trading Buddy Meyer to Boston was the "dumbest mistake" he had ever made. Griffith proceeded to trade him back to the Washington Senators for five additional players. (Courtesy of the National Baseball Hall of Fame.)

Moe Berg was a catcher for the Washington Senators during the 1920s. He is remembered best for his clandestine activities as a federal government spy and not for his catching abilities. He was a Columbia Law School graduate, and so he was one of the most educated ballplayers in history. (Courtesy of the National Baseball Hall of Fame.)

Five

U.S. PRESIDENTS
AND THE
JEWISH COMMUNITY

God gives wisdom to the wise.

—The book of Daniel

No other Jewish community in this great nation can claim a closer relationship to the president of the United States than the Jews of Washington, D.C. This relationship started with Pres. Franklin Pierce, who in 1856 signed a bill that was sent to him, approved by Congress, granting the Jews of Washington D.C. permission to build the first synagogue in the nation's capital. Washingtonians, both Jews and non-Jews, know that synagogue as the Washington Hebrew Congregation, which thrives in the District of Columbia to this day.

Among the immigrants who fled Germany during the mid-1800s was Simon Wolf. He was fascinated by politics and therefore moved to Washington in 1862. However, as legend has it, Wolf, who became an active member and early president of the Washington Hebrew Congregation, was an admirer of Lincoln. Wolf received a message that a boy from his native Ohio was to be shot for desertion during the Civil War. Wolf was able to get an audience with President Lincoln himself. Wolf pleaded for the boy's life, but Lincoln at first refused the request. Wolf then questioned what Lincoln would do if his dying mother summoned him to her bedside. Lincoln was so moved by Wolf's plea that he spared the boy's life. After this, Wolf seemed to be the minister without portfolio who represented the Jews and influenced every president from James Buchanan to Woodrow Wilson.

At the cornerstone laying of the Jewish Community Center, which took place on May 3, 1925, Calvin Coolidge delivered these words, "The Jewish faith is predominantly the faith of liberty. . . . Every inheritance of the Jewish people, every teaching of their secular history and religious experience, draws them powerfully to the side of charity, liberty and progress."

In this picture, Calvin Coolidge addresses those gathered at the cornerstone laying of the Jewish Community Center of Washington, D.C., at Sixteenth and Q Streets NW on May 3, 1925.

The front cover of this book shows the cornerstone being put in place. (Courtesy of the Jewish Historical Society of Greater Washington.)

American Mizrachi was a Zionist organization and remains so today. Mizrachi fought for the observance of the Sabbath in Israel and to preserve the religious nature of Jewish holidays in the United States. Calvin Coolidge is standing in the front row sixth from the left. Rabbi Gedalia Silverstone was the rabbi of Ohev Shalom Congregation during the 1920s and later became the rabbi of Tifereth Israel when he returned from Palestine in the 1930s. Rabbi Silverstone is standing four men to the left of President Coolidge. Ten men to the left of President Coolidge is Morris Garfinkle. This picture was taken at the White House on November 8, 1926. Coolidge was nicknamed "silent Cal" since he rarely spoke in the presence of company, but he loved to participate in special events in Washington. Six months prior to this picture, the president spoke at the cornerstone laying at the Jewish Community Center of Greater Washington. (Courtesy of Leslie Silverstone.)

Simon Wolf knew every president from James Buchanan to Woodrow Wilson personally. He was a leading member of the Washington Hebrew Congregation.

Pres. Franklin Pierce, seen here, signed a bill into law granting permission for the Jews to have a synagogue in the nation's capital.

FRANKLIN PIERCE
Fourteenth President of
The United States.
Born Nov. 23, 1804.
Inaugurated March 4, 1853.
Died 1864.

Pres. Ulysses S. Grant, as a gesture of good will to Simon Wolf, attended the dedication of the Adas Israel Congregation in 1876. President Grant attended the ceremony with his son and prominent members of his administration.

Pres. William McKinley attended the laying of the cornerstone of the Washington Hebrew Congregation on September 10, 1897. He brought his entire cabinet with him. Pictured here is President McKinley with his cabinet of advisors.

Herbert Hoover is testing the newly introduced radio. President Hoover would listen to the radio during World War II to get information as to the progress of the war. He no doubt heard on radio reports of Jews being systematically exterminated by Hitler and the SS.

President Hoover was a humanitarian and was said to be outraged over Nazi Germany's treatment of the Jews. Hoover was a signatory of the rare and unusual document shown here, which was the first public acknowledgment of Jews being exterminated.

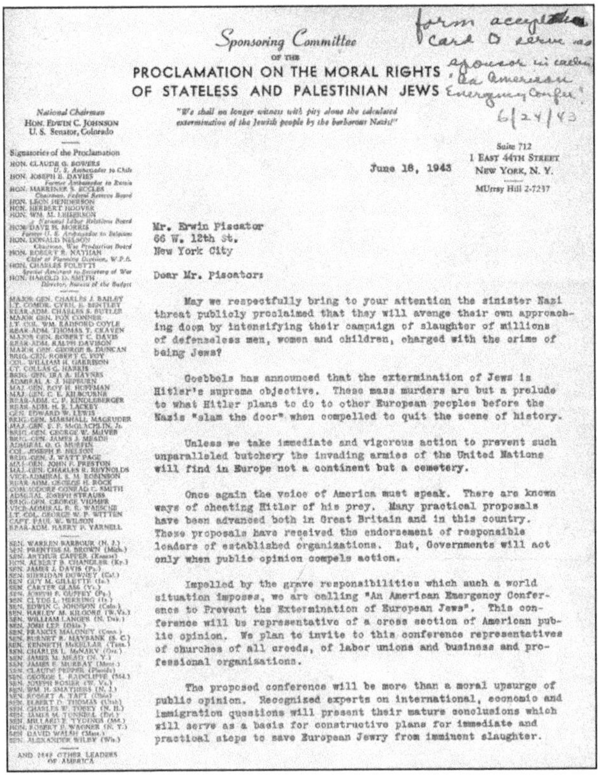

Sponsoring Committee
OF THE
PROCLAMATION ON THE MORAL RIGHTS
OF STATELESS AND PALESTINIAN JEWS

"We shall no longer witness with pity alone the calculated extermination of the Jewish people by the barbarous Nazis!"

6/24/43

National Chairman
HON. EDWIN C. JOHNSON
U. S. Senator, Colorado

Signatories of the Proclamation
HON. CLAUDE G. BOWERS
U. S. Ambassador to Chile
HON. JOSEPH E. DAVIES
Former Ambassador to Russia
HON. MARRINER S. ECCLES
Chairman, Federal Reserve Board
HON. LEON HENDERSON
HON. HERBERT HOOVER
HON. WM. M. LEISERSON
National Labor Relations Board
HON. DAVE H. MORRIS
Former U. S. Ambassador to Belgium
HON. DONALD NELSON
Chairman, War Production Board
HON. ROBERT R. NATHAN
Chief of Planning Division, W.P.B.
HON. CHARLES POLETTI
Special Assistant to Secretary of War
HON. HAROLD D. SMITH
Director, Bureau of the Budget

MAJOR GEN. CHARLES J. BAILEY
LT. COMDR. CYRIL E. BENTLEY
REAR-ADM. CHARLES S. BUTLER
MAJOR GEN. FOX CONNER
LT. COL. WM. RADFORD COYLE
REAR-ADM. THOMAS T. CRAVEN
MAJOR GEN. ROBERT C. DAVIS
REAR-ADM. RALPH DAVISON
MAJOR GEN. GEORGE B. DUNCAN
BRIG.-GEN. ROBERT C. FOY
COL. WILLIAM H. GARRISON
LT. COLLAS G. HARRIS
BRIG.-GEN. IRA A. HAYNES
ADMIRAL A. J. HEPBURN
MAJ. GEN. ROY H. HOFFMAN
MAJ. GEN. C. E. KILBOURNE
REAR-ADM. C. P. KINDLEBERGER
REAR-ADM. H. E. LACKEY
GEN. EDWARD W. LEWIS
BRIG.-GEN. MARSHALL MAGRUDER
MAJ.-GEN. E. P. McGLACHLIN, Jr.
BRIG.-GEN. GEORGE W. McIVER
BRIG.-GEN. JAMES J. MEADE
ADMIRAL O. G. MURFIN
COL. JOSEPH E. NELSON
BRIG.-GEN. J. WATT PAGE
MAJ.-GEN. JOHN F. PRESTON
MAJ.-GEN. CHARLES R. REYNOLDS
VICE-ADMIRAL S. M. ROBINSON
REAR-ADM. GEORGE H. ROCK
COMMODORE CONRAD C. SMITH
ADMIRAL JOSEPH STRAUSS
BRIG.-GEN. GEORGE VIDMER
VICE-ADMIRAL R. R. WAESCHE
LT. COL. GEORGE W. P. WITTEN
CAPT. PAUL W. WILSON
REAR-ADM. HARRY E. YARNELL

SEN. WARREN BARBOUR (N. J.)
SEN. PRENTISS M. BROWN (Mich.)
SEN. ARTHUR CAPPER (Kansas)
HON. ALBERT B. CHANDLER (Ky.)
SEN. JAMES J. DAVIS (Pa.)
SEN. SHERIDAN DOWNEY (Cal.)
SEN. GUY M. GILLETTE (Ia.)
SEN. CARTER GLASS (Va.)
SEN. JOSEPH F. GUFFEY (Pa.)
SEN. CLYDE L. HERRING (Ia.)
SEN. EDWIN C. JOHNSON (Colo.)
SEN. HARLEY M. KILGORE (W.Va.)
SEN. WILLIAM LANGER (N. Dak.)
SEN. JOSH LEE (Okla.)
SEN. FRANCIS MALONEY (Conn.)
SEN. BURNET R. MAYBANK (S. C.)
SEN. KENNETH McKELLAR (Tenn.)
SEN. CHARLES L. McNARY (Ore.)
SEN. JAMES M. MEAD (N. Y.)
SEN. JAMES E. MURRAY (Mont.)
SEN. CLAUDE PEPPER (Florida)
SEN. GEORGE L. RADCLIFFE (Md.)
SEN. JOSEPH ROSIER (W. Va.)
SEN. WM. H. SMATHERS (N. J.)
SEN. ROBERT A. TAFT (Ohio)
SEN. ELBERT D. THOMAS (Utah)
SEN. CHARLES W. TOBEY (N. H.)
SEN. JAMES M. TUNNELL (Del.)
SEN. MILLARD E. TYDINGS (Md.)
HON. ROBERT F. WAGNER (N. Y.)
SEN. DAVID WALSH (Mass.)
SEN. ALEXANDER WILEY (Wis.)

AND 2848 OTHER LEADERS OF AMERICA

Suite 712
1 EAST 44TH STREET
NEW YORK, N. Y.
MUrray Hill 2-7237

June 18, 1943

Mr. Erwin Piscator
66 W. 12th St.
New York City

Dear Mr. Piscator:

May we respectfully bring to your attention the sinister Nazi threat publicly proclaimed that they will avenge their own approaching doom by intensifying their campaign of slaughter of millions of defenseless men, women and children, charged with the crime of being Jews?

Goebbels has announced that the extermination of Jews is Hitler's supreme objective. These mass murders are but a prelude to what Hitler plans to do to other European peoples before the Nazis "slam the door" when compelled to quit the scene of history.

Unless we take immediate and vigorous action to prevent such unparalleled butchery the invading armies of the United Nations will find in Europe not a continent but a cemetery.

Once again the voice of America must speak. There are known ways of cheating Hitler of his prey. Many practical proposals have been advanced both in Great Britain and in this country. These proposals have received the endorsement of responsible leaders of established organizations. But, Governments will act only when public opinion compels action.

Impelled by the grave responsibilities which such a world situation imposes, we are calling "An American Emergency Conference to Prevent the Extermination of European Jews". This conference will be representative of a cross section of American public opinion. We plan to invite to this conference representatives of churches of all creeds, of labor unions and business and professional organizations.

The proposed conference will be more than a moral upsurge of public opinion. Recognized experts on international, economic and immigration questions will present their mature conclusions which will serve as a basis for constructive plans for immediate and practical steps to save European Jewry from imminent slaughter.

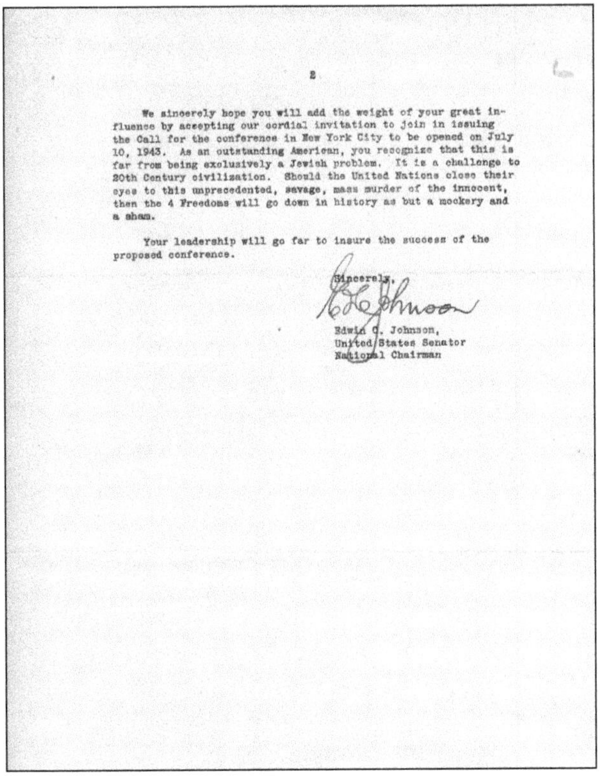

2

We sincerely hope you will add the weight of your great influence by accepting our cordial invitation to join in issuing the Call for the conference in New York City to be opened on July 10, 1943. As an outstanding American, you recognize that this is far from being exclusively a Jewish problem. It is a challenge to 20th Century civilization. Should the United Nations close their eyes to this unprecedented, savage, mass murder of the innocent, then the 4 Freedoms will go down in history as but a mockery and a sham.

Your leadership will go far to insure the success of the proposed conference.

Sincerely,

Edwin C. Johnson,
United States Senator
National Chairman

This is a continuance of the Hoover document. Maryland senators George Radcliffe and Millard Tydings were on this letterhead.

The Talmud Torah Dinner took place on May 14, 1940. Because Jews in 1940 were very pro-Democrat and pro-Roosevelt, this picture of Pres. Franklin D. Roosevelt was used in the dinner journal. Talmud Torah was the first synagogue in the Southeast of Washington, D.C.

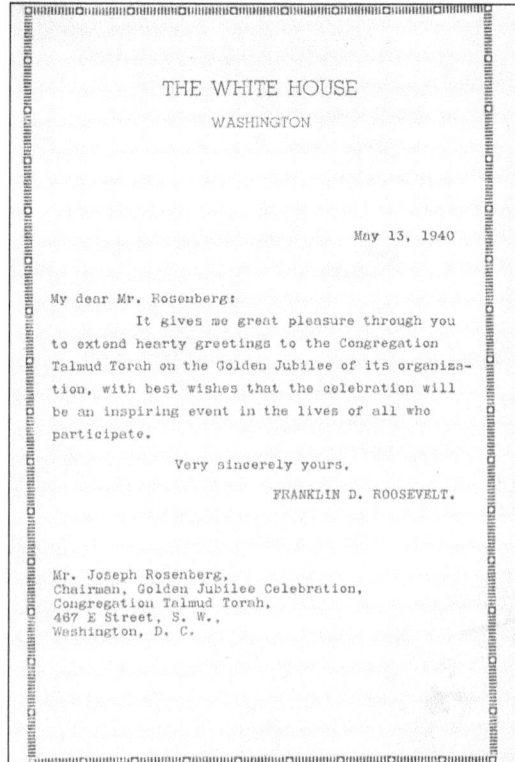

THE WHITE HOUSE

WASHINGTON

May 13, 1940

My dear Mr. Rosenberg:

It gives me great pleasure through you to extend hearty greetings to the Congregation Talmud Torah on the Golden Jubilee of its organization, with best wishes that the celebration will be an inspiring event in the lives of all who participate.

Very sincerely yours,

FRANKLIN D. ROOSEVELT.

Mr. Joseph Rosenberg,
Chairman, Golden Jubilee Celebration,
Congregation Talmud Torah,
467 E Street, S. W.,
Washington, D. C.

Written on May 13, 1940, this letter was sent by President Roosevelt to Talmud Torah in honor of its golden anniversary.

Pres. Harry Truman breaks ground at the Washington Hebrew Congregation on Macomb Street and Massachusetts Avenue on November 16, 1952.

Pres. Dwight D. Eisenhower is pictured here at the dedication ceremony of the new building of the Washington Hebrew Congregation at Macomb Street.

At different times, both Pres. Ronald Reagan and George H. W. Bush sent letters to the Ohev Shalom Congregation acknowledging the synagogue's anniversary.

THE WHITE HOUSE

WASHINGTON

April 10, 1986

I am delighted to extend cordial greetings to all
attending the 100th anniversary celebration of the
Ohev Sholom Talmud Torah Congregation.

Through the decades your synagogue's rabbinical and
lay members have become synonymous with Washington's
Orthodox Jewish community leadership. Starting as two
separate houses of worship, your congregational merger
resulted in community-wide programs and services
whose trademark was strong traditional commitment
to your ancient faith.

Rabbi Joshua Klavan, of blessed memory, and now
Rabbi Hillel Klavan and Reverend Ernest Friedman,
have been models for thousands of Jewish
Washingtonians by their exemplary lives and
unshakeable beliefs in the biblical charge: Thou shalt
love thy fellow man as thou lovest thyself. Your
encouragement to those who seek to maintain their
beliefs, and your support for the basic principles of
mutual respect and tolerance upon which this nation was
built helps ensure the freedom and vitality of our
Republic.

Nancy joins me in wishing you a memorable evening.
We send you a hearty Mazel Tov as you mark this
milestone, and a special shalom to our friends,
Ambassador and Mrs. Meir Rosenne.

God bless you.

Ronald Reagan

Pictured here is the letter that was sent to Ohev Shalom Congregation by Pres. Ronald Reagan.
Ohev Shalom is quite proud that they have had a relationship with presidents. They currently
call themselves "the National Synagogue." The original copy of this letter now hangs in the
Ohev Shalom Archives on Sixteenth Street NW.

March 18, 1991

Dear Friends:

Barbara and I are delighted to send our
congratulations as you celebrate the 105th
anniversary of Ohev Sholom Talmud Torah
Congregation.

We can all rejoice in what your house of
worship has meant to its members. A place
of prayer, fellowship, reflection, and renewal,
it has also been the focal point for many acts
of generosity and service to others. Indeed,
because the faith and values nurtured within
its walls are the foundation of strong families
and communities, your synagogue has been a
source of strength for our entire country.

You have our best wishes for a joyous
celebration.

Sincerely,

George Bush

Ohev Sholom Talmud Torah Congregation
Washington, D.C.

The synagogue was thrilled to receive this letter from Pres. George H. W. Bush. It was sent with a personal picture of him (not shown) and was signed personally by President Bush and not by autopen. He obviously recognized the importance of Ohev Shalom being the "National Synagogue," as it calls itself today. This document hangs proudly in the archives of Ohev Shalom Talmud Torah Congregation. (Courtesy of Ohev Shalom Talmud Torah Congregation.)

Six

AFRICAN AMERICANS
AND THE JEWS

And you shall love thy neighbor as you love yourself.

—The Bible

After the Civil War, the African American population migrated to the Northern cities. These folks were looking to escape the memories of slavery, racial discrimination, and economic disadvantage. When many African Americans arrived in Washington, D.C., from states in the South, they erroneously thought that they would be granted protection from the federal government. Instead they were confronted with same problems they tried to escape. More unconscionable, the federal government did little to help or protect them until the civil rights movement of the 1960s. The swell of the black population settled in Southwest Washington along the swamps of Tiber Creek where docks and warehouses were situated. Some employment opportunities for African Americans were to be found there. The early Jews of Washington, D.C., tended to settle in the Southwest of the city in proximity to the African American population.

As time passed, the Jews became more affluent, while many African Americans failed to thrive. Surprisingly and tragically, African Americans were discriminated against and lived in what amounted to segregated neighborhoods in the District of Columbia. When economic opportunities are lacking, the crime rate sometimes increases. Looking to escape crime and to elevate their social status, the Jews of Washington, D.C., moved out of neighborhoods that became predominately black.

Evidence exists that the Jews of Washington, D.C., were sympathetic to the plight of their African American neighbors. Many Jewish merchants openly welcomed them to shop in their stores, and others were employed by Jews who owned garment and millinery industries. However, socialization with their African American neighbors was kept at a minimum since Jews tended to clan together to protect and maintain their religious identity.

The archives of the Jewish Community Council of Washington, now reposed at George Washington University, support the notion that the Jews were aware of the plight of their African American brothers and supported them in combating poverty and discrimination.

This *c.* 1909 postcard suggests from the Hebrew on the bottom that America was the land of opportunity for immigrants. This was not so for African Americans during this same period of time.

Dr. Martin Luther King (right) had a strong but indirect effect on the Jews of Washington, D.C. He was a charismatic leader and spearheaded the civil rights movement. As a result of his assassination, riots in Washington, D.C., followed, leaving many stores owned by Jews burned to the ground. Pres. Lyndon Johnson (left) was criticized for not taking a more forceful hand in stemming the riots. A number of Washington, D.C., Jews expressed their concern that President Johnson did exercise strong leadership both in the D.C. riots and ending the war in Vietnam.

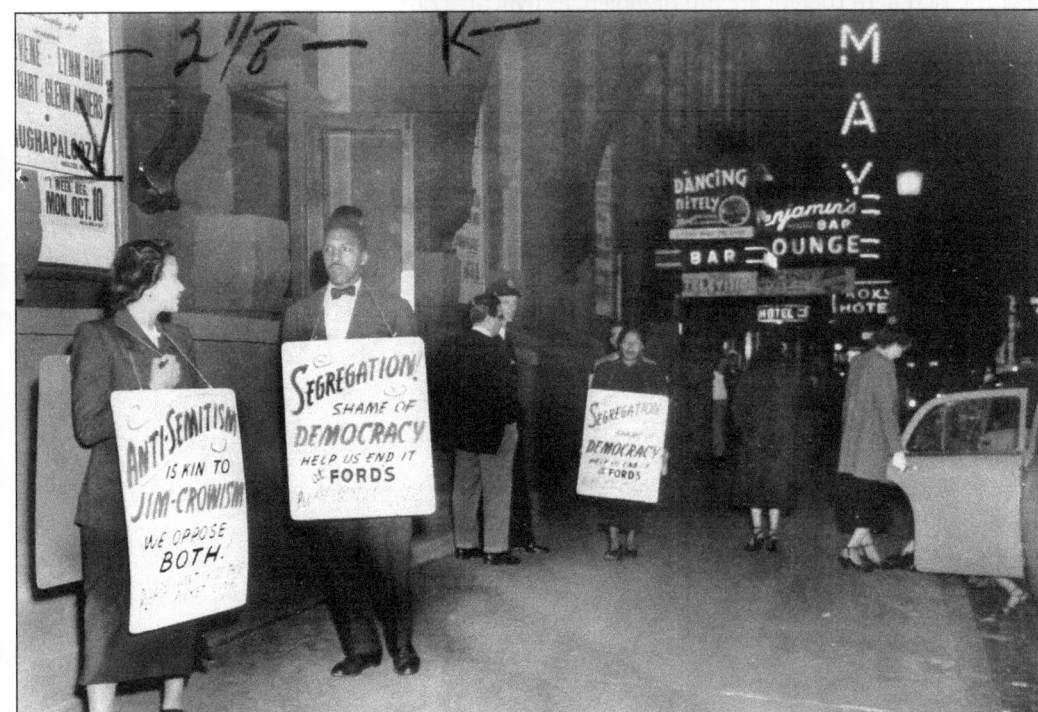

This protest took place in nearby Baltimore, Maryland, c. 1950. It clearly demonstrates that Jews and blacks could find common ground when it came to racial and religious prejudice.

Poverty is ugly no matter where it is found. This is a homeless man whose sign in Hebrew reads, "For the rich man thereof are full of violence" (Micah 12:6).

After the news came out that Dr. Martin Luther King was assassinated, riots broke out in Washington, D.C., and many stores owned by Jews were destroyed.

102

While stores were being looted, the police and National Guard stood by helpless. They were given orders not to shoot at looters since this might inflame the riots even more.

After the riots died down, workers were sent to clear the debris. It took years before all the debris was cleared away. Years later, many storeowners whose property was destroyed were given violations for debris left over from the riots. Harry Berger was issued several violations that necessitated expenses to have the debris carted off the property at 3411 Georgia Avenue. Today the property serves as a used car lot, and traces of this dry good store are all but non-existent.

The National Guard's presence made a difference in quelling the riots. Jews that served in the Guard during the riots of 1968 spent Passover away from their families.

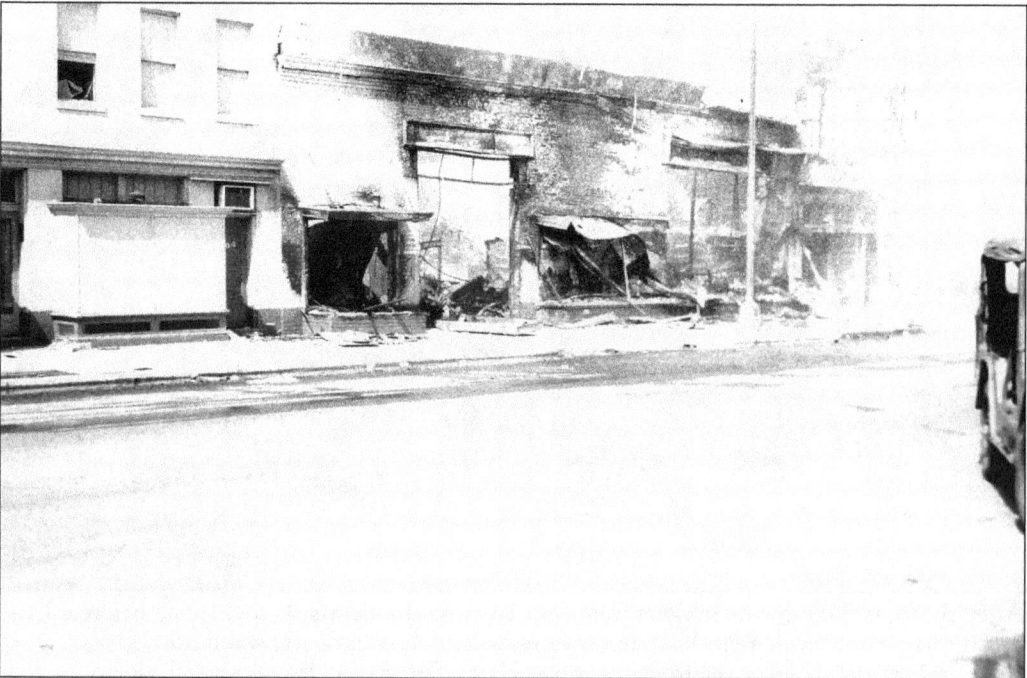

This picture depicts what was left of Harry Berger's store at 3411 Georgia Avenue as a result of the riots following King's assassination.

During the riots, many streets were closed to people and traffic. The National Guard is patrolling the street here.

Isaac Franck was the executive director of the Jewish Community Council of Washington; his tenure spanned almost three decades. He is seen here dancing the hora with Mayor Walter Washington while celebrating the 25th anniversary of Israel's independence, c. 1976. (Courtesy of the Jewish Historical Society of Greater Washington.)

ON A PERSONAL NOTE

John Norman Norris

John Norman Norris, known to all of his friends as Norman, was born on March 18, 1907, at Johns Hopkins University Hospital in Baltimore, Maryland. Norman believes he was the first black boy born at that hospital. Norman was the oldest boy of a family of six boys and six girls. His father, Samuel Norris, whose maternal grandmother was an American Indian, was a Methodist minister. His mother, Myrtle, was also a very religious person and played the organ in church.

As a young boy he grew up in Marriottsville, Maryland, located between Frederick and Baltimore. He left school early to help take care of his family. He worked mostly as a laborer on farms. He remembers working behind a plow being pulled by four horses. The dust kicked up by the horses was so great that people passing by thought the horses were loose, because little 12 year old Norman was lost in the cloud of dust.

At about age 17, Norman left home and did a variety of jobs. In 1960 he was hired to be the custodian of the new synagogue of Ohev Sholom Talmud Torah Congregation at 16th and Jonquil Streets, N.W., by the then president of the Congregation, William Rabinowitz. Norman has been with the Congregation for 26 years.

Reflecting on his many years at Ohev Sholom Talmud Torah, Norman says "I have always been treated nice . . . everyone has been friends to me." In particular, he loves the children—"They are all sweet, especially the ones raised by the hand and not the book."

Norman was happily married to the very lovely Corinthia Caroline Scott for 39 years, until her untimely death in 1975. He has a daughter, Rosi, who lives in Riverdale, Maryland, a granddaughter, Pamela, and two great grandchildren, Cecelia and Damon, all living in Washington, D.C.

Norman is a Methodist who respects how the Jewish people he has met at Ohev Sholom Talmud Torah follow their religion. At age 79, he looks forward to retiring soon.

Norman is part of the Ohev Sholom Talmud Torah Congregation family and truly liked and respected by all who know him. For 26 years the Congregation has counted on Norman to assure that its many activities are a success. The Congregation past and present thank him for his work, appreciate his efforts and wish him the very best for his future. When Norman finally retires he will be missed.

Ohev Shalom, at its 100th anniversary dinner on May 24, 1986, paid tribute to this African American Washingtonian, John Norman Norris. He was the custodian at the synagogue since 1960. (Courtesy of Ohev Shalom Talmud Torah Congregation.)

Seven

THE LEGENDARY
AL JOLSON

You ain't heard nothing yet.

—Al Jolson's favorite saying

Al Jolson was not born in Washington, D.C., as many people seem to believe. His father, Rabbi Moses Yoelson, came to this country from the town of Srednik, which was in Russian Lithuania. His family followed him. Rabbi Yoelson became the all-around leader of the Talmud Torah Synagogue in the early 1900s. He was a learned rabbi, cantor, shochet (ritual slaughterer), and mohel (one who performs circumcision of Jewish males who are eight days old).

Asa Yoelson, who later changed his name to Al Jolson, was the pride of his father in the early years. Legend has it that on the holiday of Yom Kippur, little Asa placed himself next to his father and sang in harmony with him. However, all was not well in the Yoelson home. Asa's beloved mother died when he was about nine years old. Rabbi Yoelson eventually remarried, and Asa became quite close with his stepmother as he became older.

Asa loved to play and strove to be a regular kid, but Rabbi Yoelson often disapproved of his behavior. When he was a teenager, Asa ran away with his older brother to pursue a career in show business. Harry, as his brother called himself, convinced Asa to change his name to a more Americanized name, and hence the legendary Al Jolson was born.

Al Jolson loved his father but from a distance. When it was time for Jolson to marry, he neither sought approval nor did Rabbi Yoelson approve of his marriage. Jolson married four times in his life, all to women who were not Jewish. Legend has it that Rabbi Yoelson said Kaddish (memorial prayer for the deceased) over his son upon learning that he married a non-Jew. At some point, there was a rapprochement between father and son. Jolson would visit his father in Washington, D.C., annually. When Jolson became famous, he purchased an expensive home for his parents, which Rabbi Yoelson, advancing in age, accepted with appreciation.

Rabbi Yoelson never went to live theatre to see his son perform. He did, however, see the *Jazz Singer* made into a movie, which impressed the rabbi. Al Jolson was famous for his blackface routine and for telling his life story in the performance of the jazz singer. Rabbi Yoelson is buried in the Ohev Shalom Talmud Torah cemetery on Alabama Street in Southwest Washington, D.C. Rabbi Yoelson lived a long and productive life as a Washington rabbi performing much-needed rituals for the community. Rabbi Yoelson died in 1945 while his famous jazz singer son died a mere five years later in October 1950 at the age of 64 from a heart attack.

On the right is Rabbi Moses Yoelson as he appeared in the late 1920s.

Al Jolson autographed this picture of himself, c. 1940.

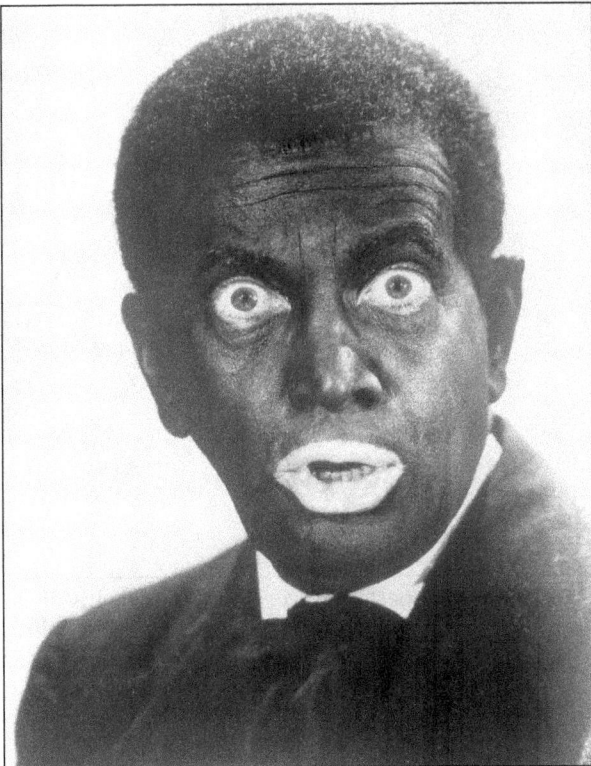

Al Jolson is pictured here in his famous blackface.

AL JOLSON IN "MAMMY" — A Warner Bros. Production

Al Jolson is shown here on stage. Jolson's most legendary performance, which mirrors his life as a young Jewish boy in Washington, D.C., is in the *Jazz Singer*. Legend has it that Rabbi Yoelson saw the *Jazz Singer* and years later admitted that he took pride in his son's accomplishment as a performer.

This is Ida Yoelson, who was Jolson's beloved stepmother. She is pictured here holding a photograph of her stepson Al Jolson. (Courtesy of the Jewish Historical Society of Greater Washington.)

Pictured here is the grave of Rabbi Moses Rubin Yoelson. Rabbi Yoelson is buried in the Ohev Shalom Talmud Torah Congregation. His grave sits quietly next to the fence surrounding the cemetery. (Photograph by Limor Garfinkle.)

Eight

ORVILLE WRIGHT ATTENDS A FUNERAL IN WASHINGTON

If I ascend into heaven, You are there.

—Psalms

The first Jewish aviator was a Washingtonian who is resting eternally in the Adas Israel Cemetery. He was a fascinating gentleman, instantly likable, and perhaps charming. Leibel Wellcher was his birth name. He came to this world during the summer of 1881 from the town of Kiev. Leibel's parents immigrated to the United States when their son was a lad of nine years old. His father died four years later, and his mother remarried shortly after the death of Leibel's father. The family moved to Washington, D.C., in 1898.

In 1901, he enlisted in the navy and changed his name from Leibel Wellcher to Arthur L. Welsh. All accounts lead us to believe that Welsh was active in synagogue and Jewish life. Arthur was a member of Adas Israel Synagogue and belonged to the Young Zionist Union where he met his future wife, Anna Harmel. Welsh was married to Anna Harmel on October 10, 1907, by the well-known Orthodox rabbi George Silverstone.

Welsh loved the idea of flying airplanes in its infancy back in the early 1900s. Welsh at first did not make admittance into the Wright Brothers Flying School when he first applied. But he was persistent and proved to be a capable airman. Legend has it that he became close to the Wright brothers, and they considered each other friends.

Tragically Welsh was killed in an airplane accident while testing a new model plane for the military, a CM-1 Wright Military Scout. On June 11, 1912, he was testing the CM-1 for its durability and maneuverability, but the plane could not endure the stress it was placed under, and it tragically crashed, instantly killing Welsh and his passenger, Lt. J. W. Hazelhurst Jr. The funeral took place in Welsh's father-in-law's house at 446 Eighth Street SW on June 13, 1912. Orville Wright and his sister attended the funeral. Wilbur Wright had passed away a short time before Welsh was killed, but had Wilbur been alive and in good health, he most probably would have joined the long list of mourners that day. The Yiddish paper in New York mentioned: "All present were in tears including Mr. Orville Wright and his sister, who were doing all they could to console the mother and wife of the deceased. Later Welsh was buried in the Adas Israel Cemetery. Welsh left a two-year-old daughter behind who grew up and relocated to England."

Both Wilbur (right) and Orville befriended Welsh and had the utmost confidence in his flying abilities. This is a rare photo of the Wright brothers posing together.

Welsh is often pictured with his hat on. Perhaps he wore a head covering out of respect for Jewish tradition, or perhaps it was a fashion statement. (Courtesy of the Jewish Historical Society of Washington.)

Welsh is seen here with his ground crew. Airplanes in those days needed constant attention both mechanically and structurally. (Courtesy of the College Park Aviation Museum.)

Pictured here *c.* 1911 is Welsh (left) sitting in the CM-1 Wright Military Scout. On the right sits Lt. Henry (Hap) Arnold. (Courtesy of the College Park Aviation Museum.)

Here is a ground crew posing for a picture, perhaps taking a break from maintaining the plane. (Courtesy of the College Park Aviation Museum.)

116

It was said that Welsh made it to his station in life out of sheer persistence. Welsh was one of five original pupils of the Wright brothers. Wilbur Wright declared that Welsh never "played to the grandstand" (showed off), and Welsh (shown here on his plane) chastised other fliers who jeopardized their lives by attempting "circus stunts." (Courtesy of the College Park Aviation Museum.)

This plane is believed to be the CM-1 shown in its completeness. In the early years of military aviation, planes had to meet demanding specifications, which, as Welsh proved, often went beyond the capacity and endurance of what the plane could tolerate. (Courtesy of the College Park Aviation Museum.)

After the plane crashed, it was transformed into a pile of debris. Welsh and Hazelhurst were killed instantly. (Courtesy of the College Park Aviation Museum.)

The plane had to withstand a loaded climb of 2,000 feet in 10 minutes. This was the last scheduled test of this plane. (Courtesy of the College Park Aviation Museum.)

As Welsh attempted to change direction while nearing the ground, the center of the plane collapsed under the stress of the maneuver. You can see the wings folded here. (Courtesy of the College Park Aviation Museum.)

The ground crew seen here is trying to straighten the collapsed wings of the plane. (Courtesy of the College Park Aviation Museum.)

Welsh is buried in the Adas Israel Cemetery. Legend has it that his body was disinterred in 1925 and then reburied in another location in this cemetery. It is a mystery why he is not buried next to his wife, Anna Welsh. (Courtesy of the Jewish Historical Society of Greater Washington.)

Anna Welsh is buried in the Adas Israel Cemetery next to her father, Paul Harmel. Anna died on January 19, 1925, and her father died in 1940. (Photograph by Limor Garfinkle.)

120

Nine

WORLD WAR II
PRODUCES HEROES

Even though I walk through the valley of death I will fear no evil. For you are with me.

—Psalms

World War II changed the face of Washington, D.C., both during the war and afterward. During the war, security measures were taken and natural resources had to be preserved. Residents remember that Russian officers visiting the Pentagon were seen dressed in uniform throughout downtown Washington during the war years.

Winston Churchill visited Washington to address Congress during the war. He made his famous speech to Congress, referring to himself as being half a U.S. citizen, since his mother, the socialite Jenny Jerome, was an American born and raised in Baltimore until she moved to England.

Washington Jews during World War II were no less heroic than Winston Churchill. During World War II, approximately 11,000 Jewish servicemen from all over the country gave up their lives for this country. The number of Jewish servicemen from Washington, D.C., who gave up their lives we can only guess, since no statistics are to be found. This chapter will briefly look at what transpired during that dark period of time.

Alexander Goode was a Jewish chaplain who perished on the *Dorchester* troop ship in January 1943. After a U-boat torpedo hit the *Dorchester*, there was chaos and panic on the ship. Goode was one of four chaplains who calmly went about assisting the men, offering them their life jackets, knowing full well that this would be a certain death sentence for them. Goode was a Washingtonian who married the niece of Al Jolson and the granddaughter of Rabbi Moses Yoelson in a simple wedding ceremony that took place on October 7, 1935, only a few hours after Yom Kippur. Rabbi Yoelson performed the wedding ceremony. (Courtesy of the Jewish Historical Society of Greater Washington.)

What made the four chaplains—George Lansing Fox, Alexander Goode, Clark Poling, and John Washington—heroes was their downright humanity and selflessness. They made the ultimate sacrifice, giving up their lives to save others regardless of race, religion, or creed. Legend has it that after they had assisted the other men aboard, these men took their last breath, locked in arms with one another and kneeling in prayer. This first-day cover shows the four chaplains locked in arms prior to the ship sinking.

Pictured here is Howard Garfinkle, a nephew of Morris Garfinkle. He was killed in action on February 28, 1945. He was in the 69th Infantry Division. Legend has it that he was killed during an assault in a town called Kamberg, Germany. His buddy next to him survived the onslaught of bullets without even "messing up" his hair. Garfinkle was 31 at the time he was killed. He was buried first in Germany, and then his body was returned abroad on the transport ship *Joseph V. Conelly*, which docked in New York on October 26. He was laid to final rest at Arlington National Cemetery. The funeral was at the Danzansky Funeral Home. (Courtesy of Shelly Wender.)

This plane was an Air Force plane possibly used in locating enemy submarines off the coast of the United States. German submarines were constantly patrolling the coast of the United States and sinking ships that were unprotected. Howard Stanley Garfinkle is in the back row, third from the left.

The late Pope John Paul II restored the Jewish life of a boy being raised as a Catholic. Shachne Hiller was a young boy when his parents were sent to a concentration camp in Poland. Mr. and Mrs. Hiller knew that they might be killed, but they wanted to save their son, Shachne. They entrusted him to a Polish neighbor, Mrs. Yachowitch, and instructed her to send little Shachne to Aunt Jenny Berger, who lived in Washington, D.C., after the war. As predicted, the Hillers did not return. Mrs. Yachowitch raised the boy as her own for the duration of the war, at the risk of her life as well as her family's. She loved the boy and wanted to keep him as her own. But plagued with doubt and indecision, she decided it best to share her concerns with the parish priest. When the priest heard the story, he was moved, but before making his decision, the priest asked the Polish woman what the parents' desires were. When this parish priest heard that Shachne's parents wanted the boy returned to his family in Washington, D.C., he said, "You must return him then." The priest became none other than Pope John Paul II.

Shachne Hiller was sent to Washington, D.C., to live with his family. As a young boy, he helped his uncle Harry Berger in the store at 3411 Georgia Avenue. Today Shachne Hiller is Stanley Berger, who lives in Stamford, Connecticut, with his family. He is pictured here at age 13, c. 1950s.

Ten

HISTORICAL MOMENTS OF JEWS IN WASHINGTON, D.C.

Make music to God and give thanks to his holy name.

—Psalms

There have been many historical moments for Jews who live in Washington, D.C. Some of these events are well known, while others are not. Some are funny and happy, while others are quite tragic. These memories make Washington, D.C., unique and special to all Washington Jews.

The legendary Andrews Sisters came to Washington, D.C., in 1940 on a short visit. They attended the Yom Kippur Ball sponsored by Bnai Brith AZA. No young Jewish person in Washington, D.C., would miss this event—short of severe illness or death. These events were so popular that advance tickets were needed to get through the door. When the Andrews Sisters appeared and tried to enter the dance, an usher inquired as to whether they had a ticket. The sisters said they did not, prompting the usher to ask if they were Jewish. The Andrews Sisters again answered no, at which point the usher was ready to escort them out the door. Sensing a problem, someone came up and said, "Do you know who these girls are, and why they are here? These girls are the Andrews Sisters and they are here to sing for us." The Andrews Sisters were then escorted inside to the gala event and sang the song that made them famous, "Bei Mir Bist Du Schon." The crowd went wild as they sang; legend says everyone had a good time.

Here couples are dressed up for the Yom Kippur Ball when the Andrews Sisters visited. The couple on the left is Howard and Roslyn Garfinkle. Fifth and sixth from the left are Erwin and Freida Garfinkle.

Philip Rabinowitz: When a Scholar Dies, Everyone Is His Relative

BY JANICE L. KAPLAN

BY RONA MENDELSOHN

"He was a patient man, the kind of teacher who let kids learn something—not just memorize," is how Ann Schiff, 7, remembers Rabbi Philip Rabinowitz.

Ann, who had been studying Hebrew with Rabinowitz on Sunday mornings at Kesher Israel, said she found it "hard to understand" why he had been murdered because "he didn't do anything to anyone."

There were many far older who were finding it difficult to understand why Rabinowitz—described as gentle, soft-spoken and scholarly—was fatally stabbed in his Georgetown home last week.

At his funeral at Kesher Israel, hundreds of congregants, Jewish community leaders, Israeli officials, students and friends crowded the

On a rocky hillside south of Jerusalem, Rabbi Philip Rabinowitz was buried in Eretz Hachaim Cemetery on March 2. Nearly 200 people, many of them former students of the rabbi at the Hebrew Academy, gathered for the hour-long ceremony.

As the group stood in the hot sun, they shared memories and wept. Shulamith Subar, past librarian at the academy, remembered the rabbi. "He was one of the warmest people I've ever known," she said. "He had a European Jewish warmth."

The rabbi's brother, Israel Rabinowitz, who emigrated from Poland to Israel in 1933, spoke in halting English. "He was a very religious

Washington Jews suffered a tragic loss on March 2, 1984, when Rabbi Philip Rabinowitz was murdered in his home. The crime is still unsolved today. Rabbi Rabinowitz was the spiritual leader of the Kesher Israel Synagogue in Georgetown. (Courtesy of Kesher Israel and *Washington Jewish Week*.)

First graders from Kehila Chadash Congregation in Maryland created tzedakah boxes modeled after Washington's historic 1876 Adas Israel Synagogue, the oldest in the capitol area. The Jewish Historical Society of Greater Washington is restoring the synagogue and hosts programs in its historic sanctuary. Listed on the National Register of Historic Places and an official project of Save America's Treasures, the synagogue is open by appointment to visitors by contacting the society.

127

BIBLIOGRAPHY

Altshuler, David, ed. *The Jews of Washington D.C.: A Communal History Anthology*. Chappaqua, NY: Rossel Books, 1985.

Banks, Ann. *First Person America*. New York: A. Knopf, 1989.

Bigman, Stanley K. *The Jewish Population in Greater Washington in 1956*. Washington, D.C.: The Jewish Community Council of Greater Washington, 1957.

Cary, Francine. *Urban Odyssey: A Multicultural History of Washington, D.C.* Washington, D.C.: Smithsonian Institution, 1996.

Clark Lewis, Elizabeth. *Living In, Living Out: African American Domestics and the Great Migration*. New York: Kodansha International, 1996.

Dalin, David and Alfred J. Kolatch. *The Presidents of the United States and the Jews*. Queens, NY: Jonathan David Publishers, 2000.

Dawidoff, Nicholas. *The Catcher Was a Spy: The Mysterious Life of Moe Berg*. New York: Pantheon, 1994.

Diner, Hasia R. *A New Promised Land: A History of Jews in America*. New York: Oxford UP, 2003.

———. *In the Almost Promised Land: American Jews and Blacks, 1915–1935*. Baltimore: Johns Hopkins, 1995.

———. *The Jews of the United States*. Los Angeles: University of California, 2004.

Eichhorn, Max. *Jewish Folklore in America*. Queens, NY: Jonathan David Publishers, 1996.

Fischer, Ron W. *The Jewish Pioneers of Tombstone and Arizona Territory*. Tombstone, AZ: Ron Fischer Enterprises, 2002.

Freedland, Michael. *Jolson*. New York: Stein and Day, 1972.

Goode, James M., *Capital Losses: A Cultural History of Washington Destroyed Buildings*. Washington, D.C. Smithsonian Institution, 2003.

Maisel, Sandy L., ed. *Jews in American Politics*. New York: Rowman & Littlefield, 2001.

Marans, Hillel. *Jews In Greater Washington: A Panoramic History of Washington Jewry For the Years 1795–1960*. Self published, 1961.

Norrell, Robert, J. *The House I Live In: Race In the American Century*. New York: Oxford UP, 2005.

Oberfest, Robert. *Al Jolson: You Ain't Heard Nothin' Yet*. London: A. S. Barnes and Co., 1980.

Passonneau, Joseph R. *Washington: Through Two Centuries: A History In Maps and Images*, New York: Monacelli, 2004.

Rabinowitz, Stanley. *The Assembly: A Century In the Life of the Adas Israel Hebrew Congregation of Washington, D.C.* New Jersey: Ktav Publishers, 1993.

Roth, Cecil, ed. *Encyclopedia Judaica*. Jerusalem: Keter, 1974.

Sforza, John. *The Andrews Sisters Story: Swing It!* Lexington, KY: University of Kentucky Press, 2000.

Thornton, Francis. *Sea of Glory: The Magnificent Story of the Four Chaplains*. New York: Prentice-Hall, 1953.

Wolf, Simon. *The Presidents That I Have known from 1860–1918*. Washington, D.C.: Press of Byron S. Adams, 1918.

Visit us at
arcadiapublishing.com

www.ingramcontent.com/pod-product-compliance
Lightning Source LLC
Chambersburg PA
CBHW050640110426
42813CB00007B/1867